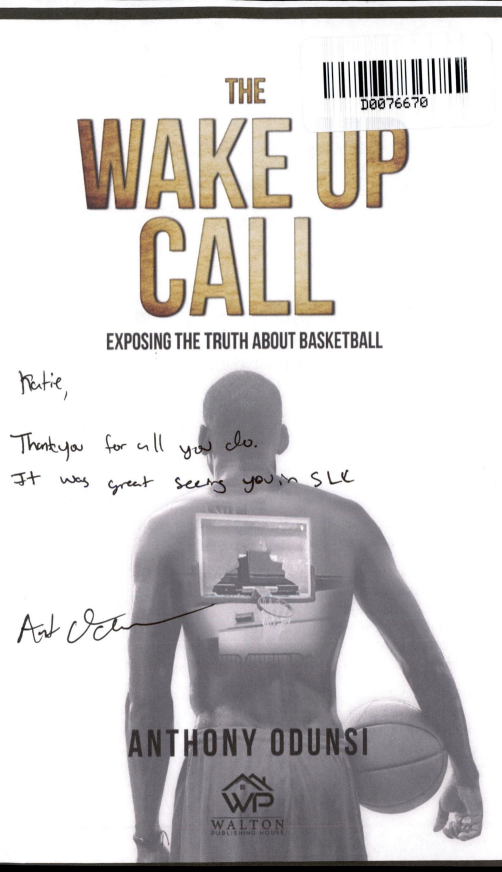

THE
WAKE UP
CALL

EXPOSING THE TRUTH ABOUT BASKETBALL

Katie,

Thank you for all you do.
It was great seeing you in SLC

Ant Odn

ANTHONY ODUNSI

WP
WALTON
PUBLISHING HOUSE

Walton Publishing House
Houston, Texas
www.waltonpublishinghouse.com
Printed in the United States of America

Disclaimer: This work is intended for entertainment purposes only. This work depicts actual events in the life of the author as truthfully as recollection permits and/or can be verified by research. Occasionally, dialogue consistent with the author or nature of the person speaking has been supplemented. All persons are actual individuals. The names of some individuals have been changed to respect their privacy. Goodluck and Godspeed proving actual malice, from the truthful recounting of the events.

The advice found within may not be suitable for every individual. This work is purchased with the understanding that neither the author nor the publisher, are held responsible for any results. Neither author nor publisher assumes responsibility for errors, omissions, or contrary interpretations of the subject matter herein. Any perceived disparagement of an individual or organization is a misinterpretation.

Brand and product names mentioned are trademarks that belong solely to their respective owners. Library of Congress Cataloging-in-Publication Data under ISBN: 978-1-7341214-8-3 herein.

In memory of Joshua Amosu
In memory of Kobe Bryant
In memory of Chief Oniya
In memory of Brent "BJ" Johnson
In memory of Garrett W. Gamble

Dedications

To Antonia Odunsi

My sister, my best friend. I know at times I may try and act older but that is just me trying to fill the void of Dad not being around. You deserved better, you deserved dad to be there but because he wasn't you are stronger, and I admire you for that. Mom always made sure we stuck together, and our relationship is a direct representation of her wishes. You have been my biggest supporter and fan. The achievements I have accomplished thus far would not have transpired without you around. Without you, there is no Anthony Odunsi. A part of you runs through my veins and I am proud to call you my sister. I dedicate this book and my life to you and mom.

To Oloori Mosunmola Adeniyi

The woman, the myth, the legend – literally. As I write these words I am as emotional as ever. I rarely cry but when I do, you and your sacrifices have always been the cause. I can't imagine what it is like raising two kids at 28, you were just five years younger than I am now when you had Tonia and me. You could have chosen adoption as an option or you could have been a horrible or mediocre mom, but you did the exact opposite and I want to let you know I noticed. You gave me life; you gave me a roof over my head and clothes to wear. You sacrificed your twenties and thirties to make sure Tonia and I had a great life. For that, no amount of money or gifts can ever repay you, and I am forever happily indebted to you.

Words truly can't describe my feelings right now; you have set the standard high and I know exactly what to look for in a wife. I don't make promises often but after seeing what transpired between you and dad, I think one is well-deserved. I promise to always be there for my wife and kids. I promise to raise my family in church as you did for us, so they will receive a Godly foundation and understand their purpose in life. I can't promise to be like you, it's honestly unobtainable and I wish I could give you an award for the world's best mom. Instead, I will start with this book. I dedicate this to you. I love you, mommy, thanks for everything.

TABLE OF CONTENTS

Foreword

It was the spring of 2012 when I met Anthony Odunsi. At the time, I was teaching basketball classes at the University of Utah and running my own skill development business. When we met, there was an instant connection between the two of us. He was finishing his first year of playing college basketball, and I was in my second year of owning my own business. One day, Anthony came to me to ask for advice because he wanted to transfer schools and needed some guidance in the process. In the back of my mind, all I could remember was the words of Lou Richie, my mentor and high school basketball coach who helped me reach my goals of becoming a Division I basketball player, saying, "Pay it forward." Therefore, when Anthony came to me asking for help, I did just that. I took that opportunity to help him as Lou had done for me, and I had promised I would do for others. I made calls and did whatever I could to help guide him in finding a school that best fit his playing style.

I connected Anthony to my former junior college assistant coach, Troy Johnson, an assistant coach at Tyler Junior College in Tyler, Texas. Anthony went on to play at Tyler, and he would later play at the University of Albany and then finished his collegiate playing career at Houston Baptist University. I instructed Anthony like had been told to me years prior, "The only thing he owed me was to 'pay it forward' to someone else," and with this book, he accomplishes that and so much more.

As all athletes know, one day, the game that we loved, the game that we ate, the game that we breathed, and the game that we dreamed of, one day making it to the professional level will come to an end. That is a tough pill to swallow. It requires having an honest conversation with yourself and acknowledge that your playing career is over, and it's time to transition.

In this book "The Wake Up Call," Anthony will share his experiences and his journey on how he had to answer that call and have that honest conversation with himself to decide to stop playing the game that he loved and how he made the appropriate steps through that transition. The experiences Anthony shares throughout this book are a great guide to athletes wrestling with how to answer the call.

Johnnie Bryant

Associate Head Basketball Coach of the New York Knicks (NBA)

PRELUDE

The motive behind the text, the deep meaning behind the letters you are about to put together to form an opinion will hopefully give you a better understanding of me, of someone like me, and the world of basketball. There isn't a single word to describe the experience, there isn't a single explanation. I consider myself and my thought process unique. Although my mindset has negatively affected me at times, I view it as a positive trait. Life is about finding your flaws, understanding how and why they're detrimental, figuring out how to own them, and making them something that others want to possess, a positive.

As you read, follow along closely to hopefully learn the life lessons to prevent you, your brothers, sons, and daughters from making the same mistakes I did. Feel free to draw your conclusion and pave your path. This is a story of my athletic experience that I decided to end prematurely, simply because I received "The Wake Up Call."

CHAPTER 1
EARLY LIFE

I believe the majority of a person's habits, morals, and ethics stimulate from their upbringing. We are all a product of our environment. What we experience at a young age is often manifested in our lives years later. It's no secret that there is a monumental disparity between races and economic status; typically between whites and blacks in the United States. On one side of the spectrum are the Caucasians; white people who have had wealth passed down from generation to generation, making up the majority of our middle and upper class. Statistically, they're the most dominant race in the United States. From CEOs of companies to business owners, a large majority of the people in these positions are Caucasians. On the opposite side of the spectrum are African-Americans; black people who make up the majority of the lower class. The Washington post states African-American people have 1/10 the wealth of white people.[1] From the beginning of blacks' oppression to now, they have always been behind. Often black parents struggle to make ends meet, living paycheck to paycheck. Consequently, this puts their youth in tough situations. Naturally, the youth find coping mechanisms. The results of this are stealing, selling drugs, or any act of quick cash to substitute for poverty, pain, and suffering.

This is the narrative in America, how unfortunate. Although to some we are equal; growing up black and Nigerian is very different. We are raised to be the first despite what statistics show. We are the most successful immigrants in the United States.[2] It was embedded in me from a very young age that Nigerians must excel. Lawyers, doctors, and engineers are the occupations of choice, and anything else, you are considered an outcast; a failure. Growing up as a Nigerian wasn't easy, there was a lot of pressure that built my

---

[1] Calvin Schermerhorn, Why the Racial Wealth Gap Persists, More Than 150 Years After Emancipation, The Washington Post, June 19, 2019, https://www.washingtonpost.com /(Accessed January 1, 2021)

[2] Molly Fosco, The Most Successful Ethnic Group In The U.S. May Surprise You, OZ A Modern Media Company, June 7, 2018, www.ozy.com)/ (Accessed January 1, 2021)

character.

I was born in Dallas, Texas, on July 7th, 1992. I was three months premature and weighed less than four pounds. There are many different complications that can cause a woman's body to deliver a baby early. My mom didn't have any of those, instead my dad physically made me come out of her womb early. He found out she was pregnant, and he beat her, knocking out her two front teeth. My mom is 5'5" light skin and a kind-hearted Nigerian woman. She has her moments, apparently, it's a Gemini thing but more than anything she wanted her kids to have everything she didn't. The family was always her top priority. On the other hand, my dad stood around 6'5", strong and obnoxious. My early life with my father was a blur, I don't remember much of him. I bet if you asked him, he wouldn't remember much about me either. He wasn't around nor did he care to be. Despite his and my mom's relationship, I don't have any reservations toward him. Memories are like customer service; you can have millions of happy customers but when one customer is unhappy, that unhappy experience can be detrimental to the company. The information will be spread, documented, and if bad enough relayed to others. Just like customer service, the only memories of my parents' relationship are unpleasant, to say the least, and those thoughts will stay ingrained in my head till I take my last breath. There are a lot of memories I can't speak of, pictures I can't delete, from moments I remember. Seeing and hearing a woman physically beaten took a toll on me, but I wouldn't figure that out for a couple of years after the fact. We think what we see doesn't affect us, when in fact everything we see has consequences, the mind is a powerful tool. I have no memory of my mom and dad together, being happy or physically touching each other in a positive way. I really can't recall when exactly they split, maybe it's because I didn't know what them being together looked like.

My mom came from Nigeria at age 17. There are more opportunities in the United States, so many Nigerians who could afford to do so would come over to partake in the American education system. While attending school she worked part-time jobs at fast-food restaurants. She had given birth to my sister and me by the age of 25, along with the responsibility of looking after someone else's kid who was in the same situation as her but couldn't handle the burden. I had an older cousin named Kenneth, not my actual cousin but like family, so it's the only title relatable. How exactly my mom took care of all three of us is amazing, she is truly my hero. After the divorce finalization, we moved into a townhome in the southwest of Houston, in a neighborhood called Alief. A community comprised of minorities, mainly African-Americans. She tried to keep us in a private school as long as she could, but due to her being the only provider, we were forced to change from private to public. I ended up attending a school called, Liestman Elementary and my sister went to a school called, Youngblood Intermediate School, no pun intended. We weren't there long. We had to leave in the middle of the year when one day after school I saw caution tape covering the entrance to our home. When we arrived at the entrance of our apartments, I saw a crowd of residents and standing there, looking frantic and afraid were my mom and sister. I sprinted off the bus and fearfully buried my head in my mother's chest. Turning my head 360 degrees, I tried to figure out what was wrong. I saw the most important people in my life, so I relaxed. Quickly, it became apparent in the complex was a fugitive hiding from the police. I wasn't fully aware of the situation but as I saw a helicopter and news reporters rush to the scene, I realized the severity. There were at least 20 cops on-site, all standing in various spots around the residency with guns held high and pointed in the direction of his home. The chief officer reiterated to him to come down and turn himself in. Surely, with nowhere to run he surrendered and was detained by the police. We later learned that he had embezzled drugs. Shaken by the entire experience, my mom moved us to the opposite side of town; New Territory. A suburb with less criminal activity, a better education system, and more opportunities. A community consisting of mostly Caucasians would become my new home.

CHAPTER 2
NEW TERRITORY

At the age of nine I started school at Brazos Bend Elementary. I was in third grade and my sister in the fifth grade. Despite my preconceived notions, I enjoyed the transition. The area was nice and very affluent. An NBA star by the name of Charles Barkley lived in the vicinity, just to put in perspective the type of people that were residential owners. I embraced all aspects of the transition, I ended up meeting a kid who would become my best friend for years, Andrew Onyebuchi. Andrew was also a Nigerian kid, we were about the same height, age, color and we both came from single-parent families. We were inseparable, it was easy to relate to him. It was like looking at myself in a mirror. We both being tall, naturally gravitated toward basketball. Nothing serious we just played around at recess. Recess was like a fraternity for young kids. Unlike when in Alief, I was an elite athlete in New Territory. I was tall and naturally more gifted than most kids. My lack of knowledge was compensated by my athleticism. It wasn't only basketball, we played football, soccer, and Four square. Young and playful, all we cared about was lunch and recess. Even on the weekend we would all call each other on our landline phones, meet at the school, and play for hours despite the weather.

I was a bit younger than all my friends; just a few months difference. Even though I didn't lack size physically, mentally I knew I was a bit immature. I didn't care about my grades. It got so bad, one year we had a statewide standardized test called the "TAKS Test." After hours of taking it, I became lazy and bubbled in random answers just to get it over with. I came to know that this test covered the entire course material of the year, students were required to pass it to get promoted to the next grade. I didn't take it as seriously as I should have and as a result, I ended up failing and taking summer school to avoid being held back and repeating the grade. Nonetheless, elementary was fun, and I adapted well to our new location. As I got older things got interesting.

Everyone in my neighborhood went to Sartartia Middle School (SMS). My sister was two grades ahead, I knew having her there would be cool. Middle school was a completely different dynamic from elementary. I had to focus more on my organizational skills. The only problem was I didn't have any. I went from elementary, which consisted of being in one homeroom for a full day to middle school where I had seven different classes which were all an hour duration. I enjoyed it because I was bored easily, the dynamics of the class structure kept me entertained. I was able to see different people and experience different teachers. I had anxiety every day while going to school because there was so much going on. I ended up running for the student council body president and was elected by my peers.

The student council was an extracurricular activity where only three students were elected to share ideas, interests, and concerns of the student body with teachers and principals. We were the students who the others felt could best represent their requests and demands. When much is given, much is required. Unfortunately because of my grades, I lost my position. I was not doing well in school and focused on everything but what I was sent to school for. I struggled with my organizational skills. I would lose papers, pencils, and assignments on a daily. I was the student who would be lost the day the assignment/paper was due and would eventually find the incomplete paper crumpled up in the back of my backpack. I was young, immature, and I didn't care that there were consequences for my behavior. At one point I was failing four of my seven classes. We only had five core classes, so that should put things in perspective.

One afternoon, I got a letter saying that my mom would pick me up early. I didn't have a phone at the time, so I couldn't ask for a reason. When I got in the car my mom looked a bit sad, but I didn't ask her why she looked that way. I just said, "Hi," and hugged her. I was quizzical on why I got pulled out of class early and if it was so urgent why wasn't my sister there also. My mom had Chick-fil-A waiting for me in the front seat, it was my favorite food. We ran some errands and then went home. I was still confused about the purpose of being pulled out of school, but at that age not going to school is a gift, so I didn't ask. Later that evening my mom called me downstairs and looked at me with a long face and watery eyes. She tried twice to speak to me but she just held me with tears rolling down her face. With a cracking voice, she said that I would not be going back to Sartartia tomorrow, rather I would be attending Grand Parkway Christian Academy, a school I never heard of. I was in shock and disbelief and immediately started crying. Completely confused, I wondered how this was even possible. Because my dad wasn't around, my mom was tough on me, and always told me the truth. She explained to me how earlier that day she was in a meeting with five teachers from my school, who were all white ladies. A couple of my teachers and a principal. They went into detail about getting me some assistance, they thought I had a problem; a learning disability. I respected them for trying to get me help, but I didn't respect the fact that they tried to diagnose me when that wasn't in their job description. I'm sure it was the hardest thing to tell someone's parent, that a part of them, something they created, isn't fully competent. My mom knew I was fine, she said, "When it comes to video games, he will master them in a week. I know nothing is wrong with my son." She cried telling me about her experience, how she felt so isolated and alone in a room with all those women.

Not only did she change my school in the middle of the year, but she also held me back a grade. Yes, I left the sixth grade in the middle of the year to attend a private school to be held back to fifth grade. This was social suicide. Private schools could bend the rules a little, so it was no problem for them to make it happen. I kicked, cried, and screamed all night. I couldn't believe this was happening. This was a transformational day in my life. It was my first "wake up call," the first moment I experienced a significant change in my life. This could have been prevented if I had just focused more, once the transition took place there was no looking back.

Chapter 3
Grand Parkway
Christian Academy

The next morning, I was enrolled at Grand Parkway Christian Academy (GPCA). A school consisting of about seventy kids, with only twelve students in the entire fifth grade. This wasn't unusual for most private schools. The teachers' undivided attention to each student is what allowed the students to excel, it was a major advantage and a reason why most parents enrolled their kids there. I cried for weeks, pouted, and complained until one day I realized that complaining wasn't getting me anywhere. I needed to figure out how to get out of that school and get back to SMS with my real friends. I would come home and play outside for hours, while others would do homework. I realized I had to change my mentality, and I did. I started to take school seriously. The education system makes people believe they can distinguish the intelligent from the unintelligent when in reality making good grades is more about an individual's work ethic.

My mom made a lot of sacrifices for us, I'm sure many of those moments went over my head but this one memory was apparent. It occurred as I was playing outside with my next-door neighbor. I was surprised by our encounter because one day we were best friends, and the next day he was making fun of me because his family had more money than mine did. He was a white kid who was influenced by his parents as we all were during our earlier years. There was a lot of this going on, New Territory was filled with wealthy people who spoiled their kids because they were financially able. My neighbor had a scooter and a bike and while he would ride one, I would ride the other and that's the way we had always played and shared for a long time. Even when he wasn't around, I was permitted to use his equipment. This particular day, everything changed, and all of a sudden the kid wouldn't allow me to play with either. When I picked up the bike, he said he wanted to use it and when I picked up the scooter, he said he wanted that too. I wondered if I'd done something wrong. We were at the age where we were 100 percent influenced by our parents. Something that was talked about, would influence us and we would act on it immediately. We weren't old enough to make rational decisions on our own, so naturally, I assumed his parents must have told him about not allowing others to play with the expensive items they had bought.

Most things I would tell my mom, but I never told her about what happened that day or how it made me feel. But she must have been watching. When I went inside to watch television my mom left the house and said she would be back soon. I was going to ask her where she was going, but in a Nigerian household, we tried to keep our questions to a minimum unless we wanted a dirty slap. A couple of hours later she returned and honked her car horn, we always knew this meant to come outside. I walked outside and asked if she had something for me. She showed me a new scooter and bike. She said she didn't know which the kids liked more, so she bought both. She was watching when the altercation happened. My friend selfishly deprived me of both of his things when he wasn't using them. My friend was inside, so I made sure I made enough noise so he would come out and see my new gifts.

My mom didn't want us to feel as if we had less because of our skin color, in a community where she knew we were minorities. We had moved to an area where kids had a lot more material wealth, and I believe she felt that she had to compensate. A mother's love is unconditional, and she was willing to sacrifice even with the added weight of me being held back a year and the added expense of private school. She didn't care, she wanted me to be happy. It didn't matter if I was the smartest or the dumbest, the first or the last, I was still her son.

I started performing better in school and I began taking my classes seriously because I wanted to go back to public school. I even thought if I did well enough, I would be able to skip the sixth grade and go straight to seventh grade. My D's increased to C's, C's increased to B's, and then eventually A's. I always knew I was capable, I just had to apply myself. The private school environment was different, I could just focus on school, it wasn't a popularity contest like public school. However, my popularity quickly changed when we had a schoolwide play depicting scenes from the Bible. I didn't offer to be in it, but my teacher insisted that I would be the narrator. The narrator by far was the biggest role. I asked her why she chose me when other kids wanted the role. She said she saw something in me and from that day forward I started to feel like there was something I had that others didn't. I just needed to find whatever she saw and own it.

I had about two weeks to memorize sixty pages of script, not to mention the addition of homework from class and tutoring sessions my mom forced me to attend after school. The teacher called me aside and told me she would let me read the script verbatim because it was so extensive, that was a relief. Two weeks went by quickly and it was the day of the play. It was the first time I'd experienced a bit of anxiety. The night before I couldn't sleep, I couldn't wait to get the play over with. I didn't know if I was nervous or anxious. When school ended my mom picked me up and I had to return back a couple of hours later for the curtain call. When I returned, the other kids in the play were wearing the T-shirts that were handed out by the teacher, but I wore a suit. I had the biggest role in the play, I had to look the part. Reading wasn't my best suit especially in a room filled with parents whose kids attended our school, but I stayed confident. The play was a huge success, people laughed, cheered, and applauded. My mom cried in joy. She always told me, "When one person doubts, another person sees the treasure." Her son whom they wanted to diagnose with a learning disability, was now playing a lead role in a play at a private school, while also being on A, B honor roll. I enjoyed the spotlight, I was nervous before the play but once it was time for action, I capitalized. It was the first time I had felt the pressure to perform. I didn't know that this type of situation would repeat itself many times in my life.

Over time, I started to enjoy GPCA, like anything else it grew on me. I became more known around the school after the play. Time is always more enjoyable when you are the center of attention. In a private school, we didn't have electives like public school. There was no PE or art class. It was strictly business; you get what you pay for. One particular day, my teacher decided to let us go outside and play. Playing outside for a kid my age was like giving grown ups money; there's nothing better in the world. There were only six males in our class, we went from one sport to the next while drenched in sweat. Playing outside was a luxury for us so we had to take advantage. The last game we played was basketball. I had played from time to time but just for fun. Around this time in my life, I started to like girls and I wanted to perform well in front of them. Girls didn't enjoy recess as much as the guys did, but they did enjoy being cheerleaders. They would cheer and clap every time someone scored. This was the day that sparked my interest in basketball. I could tell naturally I was a bit more gifted than the other five guys on the court. I scored and scored, and soon the guys on my team only passed me the ball expecting a positive outcome. Later, everyone told me how good I was. I liked the feeling and wanted more.

From that day forward I started taking basketball seriously. There was a hoop in my neighborhood where guys played all the time and I started going there after school. These guys were better, older, quicker, and much stronger than I was. I enjoyed the challenge, I knew I needed to get better. Along with evening sessions with the guys, I started going before school to shoot in the mornings. I noticed if I outworked others, there would be a positive outcome and I could surpass some of the guys who didn't put in the same effort. Nigerians are mostly about academics, usually if, that's going well, parents will let their kids engage in extracurricular activities. I told my mom I wanted to play basketball on a more serious level, so we looked into some things and found a team in the neighborhood. I was introduced to the New Territory Tigers.

CHAPTER 4
NEW TERRITORY TIGERS

M y cousin DJ who lived in the next suburb and I went to try out for the team, New Territory Tigers. Neither of us took basketball very seriously so we believed this would be the best transition. All of the players resided in New Territory where the training facility was. The moment we walked into the practice facility, I could see the intimidation on the players' faces. I didn't know any of the players since I was enrolled in a private school. That was my first organized practice, I didn't know nearly as much as I thought but an old friend always told me, "You can't put in what God left out."

DJ and I dominated the tryout and immediately they asked us to play on the team. We were a bit older than the other kids, we both were thirteen and the other kids were twelve. The only difference between my cousin DJ and I was, now I was in the same grade as all other kids due to my recent change but the DJ was a grade ahead. I knew that wasn't allowed but no one ever spoke about it. We played in tournaments against fifth-graders who were from all around the greater Houston area. One thing about being black and playing against other all-black teams while being on a predominately all-white team is that they were never jealous, they wanted us to do the work for them. At times I was convinced that their parents forced them to be out there. For some kids, their disinterest was obvious. Every time down the court one of the other players would pass the ball to DJ or me and get out of the way. It was a sight to see but overall it helped with my confidence as a basketball player. It didn't take long for people to notice DJ and me; he was very athletic, one of the quickest guards I had seen, and I was a 5'11", thirteen-year-old.

We performed well, and the coach thought we would have a good chance for national games. But all good things come to an end. During one game as we were warming up, we saw a guy on the other team with facial hair. There was an apparent age difference considering his physical features. Right then I realized how my teammates felt when they saw me because I was super intimidated by him. Most of us still had high pitch voices and we were about to play against a teenager with a full beard. We didn't know how it would end up, but we started the game anyway. This kid scored the first 11 points of the game. On his next trip down the court with the ball, I heard someone yell, "Everyone stop!!! This is not fair!!! These are just boys!!!" It was my mom; she came out of the stands and stopped the game. The coach from the other team said he knew DJ and I were older so essentially it was the same thing. The coaches told her to get off the court and she responded with, "I'm a lawyer, you will have to deal with me on Monday." My mom was not a lawyer but a mother's love for her child is unconditional and once again she came to my rescue. The coach had a fair point and DJ ended up sitting out the rest of the game. I knew everything was on my shoulders and I came up short. I didn't live up to the high expectation. I was a very chill and relaxed person, but my temper always came out when I played. I got ejected from the game because one of the kids from the opposing team was being rough. That's normal, I just didn't react to it well and that would be the narrative that would follow me throughout my career. "He's a hot head or he doesn't do well under adverse situations," were words I would hear often. Due to the rules that were the last game DJ and I played together. DJ was so good that people wanted to know who he was and where he came from. Through research, it became known that he was a grade ahead. The following week I received numerous calls from other teams. They thought I had potential and wanted me to help their team. Most coaches said the same thing but one coach stuck out. He made me feel like more than just a player, I felt he would treat me like family. That's all my mom cared about, she didn't know my potential. She just wanted me to be around good people.

Coach Will Harrison coached the Jaguars. We played against his team when I was with the Tigers and lost pretty badly- they were super talented. He had kids doing things I wish I could do. That challenged me and made me want to improve my game. I attended one of their practices and may have touched the ball just once or twice the entire time. It was different from playing with the Tigers, these guys had a different mentality and I needed to work hard and prove my worth on their team. I agreed to play with them the rest of the season, I just had to tell my coach I wouldn't be returning. Although our household lacked a male presence my mom held me accountable for my decisions. If I wanted to leave the Tigers I had to call the coach and tell him myself, she wouldn't do it for me. At the tender age of thirteen, most parents would handle such situations but my mom made me call and I matured quickly because of it. As I dialed his number, I could feel sweat dripping from my head, and I could hear my pulse. I explained to him that I was going in a different direction as DJ wasn't a part of the team. His response was soothing and gracious. He told me he knew I would eventually leave and that I had a lot of potential. I was still really sad that I couldn't play with my friends anymore. I had a fast-growing relationship with one of the players named Jake Weber. He was probably the youngest but even at a young age he understood what I went through being a minority and we became close friends due to this.

Things moved quickly and before long we were at the end of the school year. I was excited to be done with GPCA. I started to ponder about my next school ventures. I envisioned potentially attending another private school, if I was going to enroll in public school, I hoped it would be one in the vicinity of my house. One thing I felt was sure, was my mom wouldn't send me back to SMS where all my friends from the previous year were now in the 7th grade. It became obvious that we weren't on the same page because that's exactly what she did.

CHAPTER 5
SOCIAL SUICIDE

My mom no longer wanted the expense of a private school and enrolled me back at Sartartia. The first day was horrific. The first person who laid eyes on me was a girl I used to have a crush on, our eyes locked on each other and she looked at me with a blank stare with her mouth open. As I walked towards her I made a swift right turn to where the sixth graders were told to report. I assembled with the sixth graders and she went with the seventh and right then I knew it was going to be a long day. I tried to hide from as many people as I could, but it was very difficult as questions were asked and assumptions were made. It was bittersweet because I was reunited with all my friends from The New Territory Tigers, but all my friends from before I was held back were asking questions. I lied and said GPCA lost my transcripts. I don't think anyone believed it, but they pretended as if they did to my face. That year was difficult for me. I had many nights when I cried myself to sleep, it was social suicide.

Thankfully, the sixth grade flew by and I entered the seventh grade. People forgot about me repeating the sixth grade or maybe it just became old news, over time they had better things to talk about. I made sure I received good grades as my coping mechanism. I always felt no matter how well I was doing in school, people always thought I was dumb. At that age seeking validation from others was prevalent. I lacked confidence but getting held back played to my benefit not only from a maturity perspective but from an athletic point of view. It didn't become noticeable until this point.

Basketball season rolled around, and I quickly created a name for myself. I stood about 5'11", while everyone else was much shorter. It never resonated to me how playing well at sports would create a new identity. The most interesting part was that the boys were more infatuated than the girls were. Tryouts came and it was no question I was going to be on the team, I was bigger and stronger than everyone in my grade. I didn't experience the same anxiety as other players did. Tryouts included two days of waking up at 5:30 am to perform in front of the coaches. After we completed tryouts, the coaches hung up a sheet with the names of the players that made the team. There were at least seventy guys who tried out and there were only openings for twelve for A team and twelve for B team- it was brutal. I saw some of my friends who had the same love and passion as I did about basketball get cut. There was crying and screaming, it seemed like someone had passed away. We were young and basketball was all we had. For the first time in most of our lives guys got their first "wake up call." This was a well-needed wake-up call. Although it didn't directly affect me, I still realized that if a person doesn't consistently pursue something, it won't manifest for them. A lot of kids got a rude awakening that day.

After teams were selected our head basketball coach sat us all down and said, "It's not rocket science guys, we are going to give the ball to Anthony." I looked around and everyone agreed. They respected and celebrated everything I did. To them I was someone special, what they didn't know was I struggled with my identity and my ability to fit in an environment where I was a minority. The season started and I emerged as one of the best players in the district. It was amazing someone so young could receive recognition from sports. People started to look at me differently, I got high fives in the hallways and smiles from the girls. All the guys wanted me to come to their houses and hang out. I knew something was different, but I didn't want to think it was just because I excelled at a sport.

In New Territory, we received a monthly newspaper about the community affairs. One day when I arrived at school my teammates gave me a copy. I was on the front page and the story was about how good we were as a team and the significant role I played in all of it. My eyes lit up in amazement, it was the first time I was highlighted on anything. I knew I couldn't get complacent, I wanted to have more moments like that. I will never forget how that moment felt. I took that newspaper, put it in my trophy case, and prayed that it wouldn't be much longer before I had another political moment. I began playing recreationally year-round for my school and the Amateur Athletic Union (AAU). Summer basketball, also known as AAU was the league that was taken the most seriously. Kids from all over the city would compete against each other. It was costly and time-consuming. I continued to play with the Jaguars and Will was still my coach. We had built a father-son rapport over time.

AAU always kept me humble, I would be treated one way at school and then the complete opposite way on the Jaguars. Some of the players were just as good if not better, they were the best players on their middle school teams as well. Ultimately, AAU made me better and Sartartia helped build my confidence. I never attended parties, I never drank, I didn't do any of the cynical hobbies that some of the other kids were doing at my age. I always thought that to secure a spot in the NBA, players couldn't do that stuff. I believed none of the guys in the NBA ever did and that's why they were great. So, I imitated that behavior to differentiate myself from my peers.

Eighth grade was a pivotal year for me as puberty hit. I started growing underarm hair, my voice cracked, and got deeper. Our conversation amongst the guys was different as well, which led me to look at girls differently. I only hung around my teammates, it was like a fraternity. We sat at the same lunch table, talked in between classes, and even hung out after school. I grew close to two guys; Brandon Ragan and Jake Weber. Jake played on the New Territory Tigers with me, he was one of the guys who I thought was forced by his parents to play. He stood about 5 feet tall and was always the smallest out there. He used to pass me the ball as soon as he got it, maybe that's why I liked him so much. Even as we grew older, and ended up playing on different teams; our relationship remained the same. Brandon Ragan was a bully. He was wealthy, both of his parents drove luxurious cars and he lived in a house on the lake. He was also very athletic. He played basketball, football, and soccer, and was one of the best at every sport. Brandon's biggest problem was he didn't understand his privilege. Instead, he tried to use what he had against people who weren't as fortunate. He was the kid who would call everyone on Christmas and ask them what they got, knowing that their gifts couldn't compare. Although he possessed these characteristics, I was still close to him. My relationship with both of them was strong, but I was closer to Brandon. He looked like me, he was black and at that age, it was easier to relate. That year I emerged as the best player in the district and no one could compete. I quickly grew two inches over the summer, and I was about 6'1". My family discussed that I was going to be a seven-footer. I was growing so fast, even I started to believe it. Because of my physical attributes, I was dominant over everyone else in my grade.

After a game against Fort Settlement; a school in an affluent neighborhood nearby, I walked into the restroom and heard two white men conversing with each other.

"How did you guys do?"

"Man, Sartartia had this one African-American kid and he was tearing it up!"

I was happy that they were talking about me but I knew I wasn't supposed to be referred to like that. That wasn't the first experience I had with being referred to by my race. As I grew older things started to become more controversial. Kids became a direct reflection of their parents. When we were younger I never experienced much racism, besides the one incident with my neighbor, but as I became older I witnessed kids start to emulate and understand the culture that was presented in their households.

**Sartartia Middle School
Seventh Grade A-team**

Anthony Odunsi (#32)

CHAPTER 6
THE TRANSITION

Eighth grade came to an end. It was the most depressing time for a lot of kids. We knew half of our friendships would end. The suburb was split in half due to zoning and there was a new high school built which caused some changes. Half of New Territory was zoned to William B. Travis, while the other was zoned to Stephen F. Austin. I lived on the side that was zoned to Travis, a new school with only two classifications. This allowed me an opportunity to play on varsity and potentially earn some playing time as a freshman. From a basketball perspective, Travis was without a doubt the best place, but Austin was better for me socially. Both Brandon and Jake were going there.

Earlier that year during basketball season, Travis' head basketball coach Craig Brownson watched us play against Hodges Bend, the other middle school that fell into Travis' zoning. I'm sure he figured he could kill two birds with one stone; come and watch both teams and see if there was any potential. After the game, he introduced himself to me. He said he was the head coach at Travis and that if I continued to progress, I would have a chance to be on varsity. It was a big accomplishment for a freshman, to play on varsity at age fourteen, where guys would potentially be as old as eighteen. I knew I had to work hard, so I created a plan. I utilized the summer before I attended Travis to work on my craft by spending hours in the gym. I knew I had to separate myself from the others. I gave up my social life that summer and grinded on the court.

At that time I didn't know how to work smart and efficiently; I would spend four to six hours at the gym every day. I became obsessed with my craft. When I had bad days in the gym, I wouldn't talk to anyone. I would even ignore my family and friends. I took the game very seriously, I was falling in love with the process. Travis had an open gym mid-summer. I knew many of the guys who attended would play on varsity and I had to prove myself. People heard I was coming but no one had ever seen me play before. First impressions were everything, and I made sure the players who were there remembered me. I talked smack after every point I scored. "I'm 14 and y'all letting me do, y'all like this. Is this what Travis is about?"

As the youngest player in the gym, I stuck out. I knew I had a chance to be a valuable asset to them.

Travis' best player was Raymond Penn. He was already on varsity at another high school but when the zoning change happened, he was affected and had to transfer to Travis to play junior varsity for a year. I didn't know much about him nor had I seen him play, but I'd heard he was one of the best players in the city. Although he wasn't there that day, I knew the message would be relayed to him.

During the summer, I transformed into the best player on the Jaguars. I watched myself pass players up. Every time I would workout I would think about the players on my team or other players who were better than me in the city and I used them as my motivation. I was a kid that was never satisfied, it was one of my best characteristics and also my biggest flaw.

CHAPTER 7
SETTLING IN

S ummer ended and I was finally a high school freshman. The first couple of days were the worst. I became quickly overwhelmed by the large crowds at the school. I did not know where to go nor did I have any friends. Although everywhere I went people knew me because I was the freshman that was going to be on varsity, it took a while for me to settle in. There was one name I heard a lot more than mine and it was "Ray."

Raymond Penn was talented and at that time the most talented player I knew. He was 5'8" but hard-nosed and tough, super quick and athletic. The ball stayed glued to his hand, he never turned it over and he had a natural jump shot to where he could pretty much shoot from anywhere on the floor. His best quality was his confidence. He thought he was the best and that is what made him great. He was the best thing that happened to Travis, I was just too stubborn, and did not want to accept it. He wasn't a role model, but people wanted to be like him. In my opinion, it didn't matter if someone tried to do the right thing, being talented would always override that. He was one of the most egotistical players I'd ever met. He would do all the wrong things but perform at a high-level. I quickly understood the characteristics that hurt him were also what made him great. I was one of those kids with an overpowering conscience. I felt I had to be on time, pray, or even treat people right to have a good game. He just balled, with no conscience, he was a unique talent.

With only three classifications we knew it was going to be a fight. It was everyone's but Ray's first time on varsity, we were all inexperienced. But things went better than intended for me. Not only was I on varsity as a freshman but I was also part of the starting unit. The transition from being the star to becoming a role player was a nightmare. It was the first time I hit adversity and I didn't respond to it well. I was immature and selfish, and I didn't care about the team. After struggling all preseason, I finally started to find my niche. I found where I belonged, and I owned it. I played a role and instead of trying to compete with Ray, I became his sidekick. I began to get a lot of attention both around the school and around the city. I used to think the best way to get recognized was to be a single man team. I started to figure out how beneficial it was to play with good players. People came to watch, and the word spread. At the end of the season, we finished amongst the top seven teams in the league. This was good considering we didn't have any seniors and we were going to have everyone back the following year. Basketball had a period when all of the teams came together for additional practice. During the season, this time was taken very seriously but after the season coach didn't care what we did.

I walked in late one day and everyone was clapping. The district accolades came in and I'd won "Newcomer of the Year." From this point onwards my career changed drastically. Not only was it an accomplishment for a freshman to play on varsity but I won the best new player in one of the best districts at fifteen years old, this was pivotal. After that achievement, I knew the following summer was going to be big. Although I was young, I still had eyes on me. College coaches typically do not start recruiting until a player's junior year but if you're talented enough they will contact you as early as eighth grade. I decided to leave Coach Will and go to another team I felt could take me to the next level. This cycle would end up repeating itself an additional three to four times. I always felt like I needed change, one of the worst traits I possessed. Maybe I got this from my father, maybe because he didn't exhibit stability or loyalty in my life, I didn't think it was necessary. We are all products of our environment. I knew Coach Will was like a father to me, he was the reason for a lot of my success early on but I had to do what was best for me, although it may not have always been righteous to the people involved. I know more than anything Coach Will wanted me to succeed, that's the type of coach he was. He always put the players first. He saw my potential and knew I needed to play with a more reputable team. I knew I needed to move on.

I went on to play for a team called Houston Select, they were sponsored by Adidas. All of their gear was provided by Adidas and all tournaments, flights, and hotel costs were covered by a man named David Salinas. I never physically saw him, he rarely came around, but it was made apparent that he was very wealthy. Because of his generosity, my mom had one less expense she had to worry about. I intended to always make things cheaper for her. Every couple of weeks we would receive an immense amount of gear; shoes, shirts, shorts, and socks. I started to figure out, the more talented I became the more doors would open. Although we attended rival high schools, my friend Brandon and I grew closer because of basketball. We worked out together for hours, he had a great work ethic and I respected that. I wanted him to have success as well, so I took him to the tryout with me for Houston Select. Although I had received an invitation for a spot on the team, it was still an audition and I knew I had to perform. Brandon was trying to make the team, and I was trying to show the guys it was my team. They had recently hired a new coach and I didn't know much about him. He was a geeky looking white man that looked like he owned half of Houston. I thought, *What would this guy know about basketball?* His name was Jim Claunch. Our relationship transitioned from the court to personal pretty quickly. It was a great summer and basketball was enjoyable with Jim. He soon became one of the most influential people in my life. I looked at him as father figure. He called daily, he taught me how to act on and off the court. He was a father first and a coach second, all the players had a personal relationship with him.

My relationship with Brandon also grew drastically. I spent nights at his house before games, after games, and even in between games at times. After eighth grade, my mom stopped coming to my games. She was a homebody and as long as she knew I was in good hands, she was fine with giving me money for the weekend and sending me on my way. Brandon's parents were the complete opposite. They went to every practice and game. They were the parents that showed up with Houston Select shirts on, they were the ultimate supporters. Brandon's dad drove us everywhere, he made a lot of sacrifices as most parents do, but I think Brandon was too immature to see it. His dad and I grew close. I started to think all these men tried to fill a void because they knew my father wasn't around when in reality I was seeking attention from them. I had no guidance and discipline when it came to basketball, my mom was hands off at this point. These men were role models that tried to help me in any way that they could. There were times I felt Brandon's dad liked me more than his son, heck there were times I think I liked him more than Brandon.

CHAPTER 8
ON THE RISE

My sophomore year crept up quickly and expectations were high. Our team was invited to a pre-season invitational called, The Super 16. It was the top sixteen teams in the Greater Houston area. We were going to be coached by Raymond Penn's trainer, Chris Gaston. Chris was one of Houston's best individual basketball trainers. Ray took me to work out with him during freshman year. Chris quickly became a brother to me. I called and messaged him all the time. He was someone I expressed my future endeavors too. He knew what level I was trying to reach, and I trusted that he could help me accomplish my goals. The best players in Houston trained with him and if I wanted to be the best, I needed to continue to surround myself with the clientele he worked with.

We weren't one of the top sixteen teams in Houston, we just had one of the best players. We received an invitation because of Ray. The previous summer he dominated the biggest showcase of the summer, the Las Vegas Super Sixty-Four. Sixty-four teams from all over the country went to Las Vegas to play, while college coaches surrounded the gyms. There was a lot of talent and opportunity. He emerged as one of the top point guards in the country, number eight to be exact. There was a controversy between him and another Houston legend; Tommy Mason Griffin. Ray was signed to Oklahoma State and Tommy was signed to Oklahoma. This rival was the reason behind the invitation, the people who hosted the camp knew the matchup would sell tickets. We were scheduled to play them in the first round of the Super 16. I knew how much was riding on the game. It wasn't about me, it was Ray's spotlight. There was no preparation before the game, which meant no practice of any sort. It was pre-season for scouts around the city and college coaches to recruit players. It was single-handedly the most impressive basketball I had ever been a part of. These two guys had an impeccable natural talent. There were two types of talent. The God-given talent and the talent you work for. Ray had every bit of God-given talent.

The game started and there were very few people in the crowd. Fifteen minutes into the game and there were no empty seats. People were standing across the entire gym, even blocking walkways.

Although the attention was on Ray and Tommy, I quietly stuffed the stat sheet. Later, I ended up becoming one of the top five players in Houston and then went on to become one of the top fifteen players in Texas. I received a lot of attention and was recruited from schools all over the country. Things I used to pray about became a reality and it happened quickly. I was one of those kids who got a taste of success and never became complacent. I liked the feeling of success and attention, so I worked ten times harder to get what I deserved. I saw the recognition crossing over to my social life. People treated me differently because of basketball and I was thankful for that.

After the game, I was invited to an after party. Usually, I would decline but because I played well, I thought it was time for me to attend my first high school party. I also knew my girlfriend was going to be there. Her name was Madelyn, she was a 4'11" cheerleader, how ironic. This particular night I showed up to the party fully coherent. I never drank or smoked, I stayed away from trouble. When I arrived, I saw a friend from my neighborhood barely standing. His name was Bryan. He was one of those kids without an identity. He wanted to fit in, so he did things to validate himself, and that night he took some pills. He was one of my teammates from the New Territory Tigers, I cared for him like a brother. I tried talking to him, but he wasn't responsive. He couldn't stand up straight and he started foaming from the mouth a bit. I saw another one of my friends leaving the party and I begged him to take Bryan home, thankfully he agreed. Madelyn and I finally were getting a chance to hang out only for the cops to shut the party down right after and break up our plans. Everyone made sure I was the first to get out of there. I heard them screaming, "Make sure Anthony gets out," and "Get Anthony out of here," people looked out for me because they knew I had a future. I was blessed to be around people like that. On the way home, I asked my friend to stop by Bryan's house because I had a funny feeling about the entire situation. I wanted to check on him.

We pulled up to his house and I saw Bryan's face planted in the grass. My friend I told to take him home left him there and I felt partly responsible. I jumped out and tried to wake him up, hoping he didn't overdose on whatever it was that he took. He was grimacing and moaning in pain. I knew I had to get his mom. She knew me from Tiger's basketball. She seemed to be the most innocent lady around.

She was foreign, a first-generation Indian that came to America so her kids could have more opportunities. His mom stood about 5 foot, skinny as can be. My mom was a foreigner as well which made me have empathy for the situation.

I rang the doorbell, she opened the door and looked at me, "Hi Anthony, Bry—" I cut her off, and in a soft whisper I told her not to panic. I explained to her Bryan took something and I wasn't sure what it was but that we needed to get him help. She asked where he was located, and I shifted my body so she could see him laying on the grass. She started yelling and saying words in her native language. She ran in the house and brought out bowls full of water and threw it on him. "Bryan…Bryan…wake-up…wake-up" she cried. I could see the agony on her face. I offered to pick him up and put him in the shower. As I picked him up, I immediately felt he was all dead weight. I could hear my shoulder crack as I lifted him off the ground. I told her not to panic and he would be alright. Bryan's dad worked overseas, and it was just his mom at home. I knew she was alone, and she was scared so I held her like she was my mom. Shaking in my arms she said, "Thank you, Anthony…thank you." That experience made me put things into perspective, and I decided not to go out to another party for the rest of the year.

After a year of getting acclimated, the game of basketball was slowing down for me and I was having a great sophomore year. Roles on the team were defined and we were on pace to make playoffs for the first time in school history, which led us to our biggest game of the year. More for us than the opposing team. We were playing against Hightower High School, easily the most talented team in our district. They were big, strong, athletic, and they were filled with Division I talent. This was a big game for Ray, every game was. There was pressure to show why he was the top point guard in the country night in and out.

The big night of the playoff arrived. Ten minutes until tip-off, after I finished stretching and warming up, I walked back to the locker room to meditate before the game. My phone buzzed with a message from Martin Fox saying, "I am bringing Big 12 school to your game today." Martin was an ambassador for my AAU team and one of the most connected individuals I knew with phone numbers from coaches from all over the country in his phone. If he liked you and saw potential in you, he would help you. My eyes lit up. I knew I had to play well. *Go out there and play your game if you are good enough, they would like you,* I told myself.

When I was a freshman, I was told Wichita State was coming to one of my games and I played horribly. Filled with anxiety, I was worried about what they would think of me instead of just doing the best I could and then let destiny run its course. Consequently, I replied back, "Okay," to Fox and made sure I was fully focused. I made sure I was ready to reveal to people how good I was on a stage where everyone would be watching.

Earlier that day, at school I had to do test corrections. There was the teacher who was subbing but mentioned he knew who I was. He explained to me that he knew I had a game today and he wanted me to just play as hard as I could without thinking about scoring. I didn't know nor had I ever seen that teacher in my life, but I took his constructive criticism to heart. Surely, I played one of the best games of my entire life and it could not have come at a better time. I finished with 27 points and 9 rebounds. From then on, my name was in every conversation concerning our district. Maximizing the opportunity when it was given was all it came down to. After that game things escalated fast. One day I was in my coach's office telling him how I saw myself going to a small academic school to almost overnight visiting one of the most prestigious basketball and academic institutions.

The conversation changed amongst friends and family about me playing in college. Rather than "if" it was more of a "where." There are two types of college visits; official and unofficial. Per NCAA an official visit is when a prospective student-athlete visits a college campus paid for by the school. Players are allowed five in total. An unofficial visit is when a student-athlete pays their own way to the university, typically it's to bring in players who grew up or played in the vicinity. I took my first unofficial visit during the summer of my sophomore year. I didn't know what to expect because none of my peers were going on visits so I had no one to bounce ideas off of. That summer I received my first offer from Vanderbilt.

Vanderbilt is one of the countries most sought after academic programs. Although they have a very low acceptance rate, I had the opportunity to get accepted while deviating from the same stressful application process other kids went through. Basketball made this possible. I arrived at the airport and was picked up by one of the players. Typically, it would be a coach but since it was unofficial, one of the players substituted. When we arrived at the campus, I was astonished by the scenery. From the architecture of the campus to the beautiful green grass perfectly sprouting out of the soil. I fell in love with the school and it's pride. Vanderbilt's head coach called me into his office and said he was impressed and that he wanted me to play for him. I didn't understand the magnitude of what was going on. Instead of reaching out to my family to help me deal with my decision, I called Drew and Jake. I valued their opinion but since they didn't have the same opportunity in basketball, they didn't know what to say. My entire life I would always seek advice and direction from other male companions because my dad wasn't around. Everyone wanted to help but no one wanted to overstep their boundary. The more people I asked, the more confused I became. That same summer, Iowa State set up an unofficial visit and my college interest grew from there.

After a big summer, the hype started to affect my head but not to the point where I was ignorant. Ray graduated, and I was now the focal point of the team. A lot of people didn't expect us to do well, they didn't think I was talented enough to carry us. I wasn't as talented as Ray Penn. I wasn't going to dribble fifty times and make a ridiculous shot. I worked hard for everything I had. It just wasn't as effortless, so people didn't want to put me in the elite category. The good thing was, I never had to carry that 2009-2010 team. It was a very tight-knit group. It was our third year straight playing with each other. At times I had moments where the older guys bumped heads with me. I was younger, thus was favored, and I'm sure it got to some of them. Ray was so much more talented, there was no doubt that he was the best. With me, the guys on the team felt they could compete, they felt there was nothing special or unique about me.

That season was transformational for me on and off the floor. I matured as a basketball player. I hit my first game-winner and I was put in many situations that allowed me to grow as a basketball player. I was the best player. As the year went on the team looked at me during big moments. I stopped growing taller and I stood at 6'3". I knew there was a plethora of shooting guards my height so I made a change that I knew would make me more appealing to college programs. I transitioned from a wing player to a point guard and the team allowed me to do so. We had a point guard named Marc Price. He was small and quick, but he was also humble. He did whatever the team needed him to do and at times, it was for him to sit on the wing and let me make plays. I owe my smooth transition to him.

As the playoffs came into formation, we had low expectation for ourselves- we weren't the favored team, to say the least. None of our seniors had any college offers and I was still indecisive about where I wanted to play after graduation. Despite our outlook, each game buses and vans filled with students from our school came out to support us. Every game was marketed well, and Travis exhibited extreme school pride. The chanting, yelling, and screaming were electrifying, the support led us to multiple wins. Before we knew it, we were one game away from going to the state championship. The team bonded and with every win the trust became unbreakable. Our final test before going to state was arguably the most talented team in Houston. A team that consisted of five Division I's signees in their starting lineup. We were matched up against Bellaire High School. On their team was my AAU teammate Sheldon McClellan who was number one in our class in Houston, he was signed to Texas. Also on the team were Tobi Oyodeji, who was signed to Texas A&M, Kenny Anyigbo signed to Western Kentucky, Jonathan Evans signed to Houston Baptist, and Sebastian Douglas signed to Cleveland State. Teams were lucky if they had one Division I player, Bellaire had five and that was hard to accomplish in high school.

The game went down to the wire, all the way down to the last seconds of the 4th quarter, and without realizing it I used my last foul and I was forced to sit out. In came our sixth man. Having not played for almost the entire second half he entered the game and took a shot we had not seen him make all season and he missed. We were so close. It was a great game but devastating for the team and coaches. I never knew who to blame for the loss, Coach Brownson for subbing that kid in or that kid for getting a random burst of confidence. Nevertheless, we made history, Travis had never advanced that far in the playoffs and I got to be a part of it. It was a great group of guys, and the most fun I had playing basketball in my life.

A couple of weeks after the season, I made another visit to Iowa State to visit their new coach, Fred Hoiberg. Fred was a former player at Iowa State and they called him the Mayor. He was extremely popular from his playing days. He played many years in the NBA and said that I had good size for a guard but he wanted me to stick to playing full-time point guard. I took his words to heart, knowing he knew what it took to get to the next level. When I visited, they put me up in a hotel right across the street from the gym. I went in late at night to dribble around and call plays out like I was in an actual game. They had a point guard on the team who would have been graduating the year before I enrolled, so it worked perfectly. They didn't have the academics Vanderbilt did, but they were in a great conference and I was going to be Fred's first recruit. I thought we had a special bond because of it. I was told never to make decisions based on emotions but as a 16-year-old, I was gullible. Out of pure excitement from our conversations during my visit, I committed. Without talking to friends or family I made one of the biggest decisions of my life. This was a huge relief, I committed early and now I could focus on improving my game.

After I made the decision, I called my mom and told her I would be going to Iowa State and I would be a cyclone. She said, 'Iowa, why Iowa?' I don't think she understood how big of a deal it was to go to a school of that magnitude. She asked what she needed to pay for, and I said, 'Nothing.' Most people's parents would be super involved in such a big decision, whereas for me I was making them on my own. It wasn't as if my mom didn't want to help but she just didn't understand everything that was involved in making a decision like that, such as the playing time availability, location, coaching, etc.

The Iowa coaches informed me that on Monday there would be a media release. They said there would be a couple of reporters who would contact me about my signing and that would be it. Monday morning rolled around, and I had 15 missed calls and a handful of text messages before I woke-up. While getting ready for school my phone buzzed uncontrollably. I spoke with every reporter I could. I was late to school that morning and even in class, I was still getting calls with an Iowa area code. Once the news was disclosed, my phone flooded with people all over congratulating me on my decision. Some people were happy, some envious and some just didn't think I was good enough. People talked about it all week but then the news faded away and I was just another early commit of 2011.

I thought the pressure was over. I thought it was going to be a stress-free summer. I went from trying to prove to coaches I was good enough to dealing with the pressure of performing and proving to everyone that I deserved to sign to a school like Iowa State. People always had expectations, mostly this came from people who didn't play, just spectated. I received a lot of criticism, some good and some bad but I couldn't lose focus on what was important and that was trying to get better. I didn't know the magnitude of what it meant to sign to the Big 12, and the scrutiny that came with the accomplishment. My every move from when I gave my verbal commitment would be watched, followed, and documented.

The summer ran its course. I played with two other players signed to the University of Texas. In total there were three Big 12 commits on our AAU team. Our games were always packed with coaches. Although the best players were signed, they still wanted to see us play. There is a false narrative that a player needs to average 30 points to get recruited. While that is true in some cases, in most cases it was better to be surrounded by talent and fit a role because there were only one or two players who could take the shots on teams. The role players were just as essential.

Anthony Odunsi (#23) soars up and dunks the ball after being fouled in a play-off game (Junior year).

Travis High school vs Clear Springs High School

CHAPTER 9
THE FIGHT

As the summer ended and the school year approached, I was ready for the biggest season of my career. I was going to be the man of my team, but I decided to do something that would change my senior season. I heard of two players that lived in the area that was zoned to Travis but didn't enroll for whatever reason. I later heard they wanted to but didn't because I was there. I had a reputation for not passing the ball, but it was more of I didn't pass the ball to people I didn't respect. The two kids were Aaron and Andrew Harrison. At the time they were two of the most highly sought-after kids in their class and the number one point guard and the number one shooting guard in the country living under the same roof. Before the school year started, I reached out to their dad and expressed my interest in winning a championship and that to do so, I would need his sons' help. He told me he didn't know who my parents were but he respected me so much for reaching out and doing that. The next day he and Coach Brownson had a meeting. I am not sure of the specifics that were discussed between the coach and Mr. Harrison, however, I am pretty sure I wasn't included in much of it. I never thought about that decision negatively impacting me. I genuinely thought only good things could come from it. I was already signed, and I was trying to solidify myself as one of Houston's greats by winning state. After the move became official, one of my teammates who was committed to Texas messaged me and said, 'Ant, you don't even know what you did,' and from that point, I knew I was in for a surprise.

The school year started, and I quickly heard the buzz. Not the buzz about me, the Iowa State signee. Not the buzz about Travis, the team that almost went to state the year before. But the buzz about Andrew and Aaron. I didn't think much about it until one day while walking down the hallway I heard a kid say, 'That's Anthony Odunsi, he is the third-best person on varsity.' I knew the twin's politics were strong but slowly I started to realize how much clout they had.

Before the season, college coaches were allowed to watch players workout, it was called a "live period." During live period college coaches could call, visit, and recruit players. Typically, coaches would visit the juniors and seniors first because they were a priority.

But when it came to the twins, it was a different situation. The twins were sophomores during this time and technically coaches could not have spoken to them, yet they had the biggest colleges coming to see them on the first day of the live period. I couldn't fathom the thought of it. The coaches couldn't talk to them, but they would still fly out there on the first day of the live period to show their faces. I saw some of the biggest named coaches walk through our gym because they knew two years down the line the twins were going to be major assets to a college team. I realized how highly recruited they were but I wasn't envious, I just concentrated on myself. I had to figure out how I was going to play as a freshman in college and start. That season I woke up at 5 am every morning, packed my clothes, and headed to the gym to workout. I was dedicated to the grind as much as ever. After the workout, I would take a shower and head straight to class. At times I would be so locked into the workout that I would just run to class sweaty. I wanted to be great and I had to put in more work than everyone else. People respected me for how hard I worked. I led by example; it was hard for others to match my work ethic.

Travis was an Adidas gear school, as other schools in the district. Before that season, for the three years, the varsity players were provided Adidas shoes and Riddell jerseys. That year Travis changed to Nike. From apparel to shoes and everything in between we were decked out in Nike gear. *What had suddenly changed? Why was the gear switched to Nike?* I questioned. I always wondered if it had anything to do with Aaron and Andrew because they always wore the nicest Nike gear to school. Gear that was sold in stores, but colors that weren't available to the average customer. They also weren't the type to buy fake stuff.

The season took off and during the first couple of games, everyone was timid. We always won by a large margin, but no one was aggressive. No one wanted to be labeled as a ball hog when we had so much talent on one team until we played La Marque High School, and the rivalry became personal. They had one of my AAU teammates, Julien Lewis, a University of Texas commit. I wasn't the biggest fan of Julien but I tolerated him because he was my teammate. I didn't want to lose that game, so I came out aggressive. I finished the game with 30 points. Reporters and magazine writers ran up to me after the game. I saw the twins' dad upset but I didn't know why. The next day we had practice and after the twins' dad walked into the locker room. From the coach's office, our locker room wasn't visible. Coach Brownson not knowing I was in there said to Mr. Harrison while walking through the door,

'We talked to Anthony about passing the ball.'

He replied and said, 'I didn't come in here to talk about Anthony, I came to find out how to get my boys shots.'

At that very point, Mr. Harrison knew he had leverage. He knew by that comment he could take advantage of Coach Brownson and that's exactly what happened the rest of the season.

I was leaving for college and they were staying. He didn't want to lose them so everything he did was warranted. Aaron was the shooting guard. He was a bit taller than Andrew at about 6'6". He was tall and could shoot the ball. I can recall a time when he went an entire week of practice and didn't miss a shot. I believed he was the more talented out of the two. Andrew was a 6'5" point guard. It was rare to see kids his size playing that position and because of that, he was highly recruited. It was impressive to see some of the things they could do without trying. They weren't the hardest workers, but they didn't have to be because like I mentioned before, "You can't put in what God left out."

On November 17; National Signing Day I decided to sign my national letter of intent to Iowa State. Before this, Ray was the only player to sign at our school. Coach had a small presentation in the library for him, so I expected the same. Although Ray was more talented, I was a little more liked. Well, I was a lot more liked. Coach Brownson moved my signing to the gym during basketball period and kids from our school filled the stands while all the coaches wore Iowa State apparel. Jake and other important people also came to support me. I couldn't believe the outcome; I was amazed and honored that so many people cared. I gave a speech about the process it took for me to get to that point and the people who helped me along the way. Although everything happened quickly, I will never forget how blessed and lucky I was. I knew and understood there were players who worked equally as hard but did not have the same success as I did. November 17, is a day I will never forget, it will forever be embedded as one of the most vital days in my life.

The other day was senior night. It was equally as important but not as positive as it led to being the most controversial night of the year. Senior night was a night dedicated to seniors to honor and appreciate them for their time played on varsity. Oftentimes it was a senior's last game played. I was fortunate to sign and play at the next level so it would not be my last game, but I knew how blessed I was. During introductions, after my name was called as I turned around to shake the referee's hand, I noticed the crowd was more packed than usual. The gym was filled with fans, parents watching their kids and college coaches watching one of the most talented teams in the country. When the game began it was four seniors who never played and myself. Coach started all seniors to honor the night and the players for their endeavors. The other four experienced about two minutes of action until our coach pulled them out. For the first round of substitutes, coach left me in along with the twins and a couple of other teammates and we quickly went up and gained a solid lead. He made another round of substitutes, yet again left me in. It was one of my last games, he wanted me to soak up every moment. One possession I stole the ball and back tapped it to Aaron, then took off for the fast break dunk. I knew I could move faster without the ball. After I stole it, I tapped the ball in his direction so he could throw it ahead but when he received the ball, he acted as if he didn't see me. I grew furious, it wasn't the first time he'd done that. I yelled, cursed and screamed then mumbled,

'You always do that shit!'

'Shut your bitch ass up,' Aaron snapped.

I stopped at half court and said, 'What did you say to me?' Meanwhile the entire team was on the opposite side of the court.

He reiterated by saying, 'Shut your bitch ass up,' and out of anger, I pushed him. He swung back at me and missed and before I knew it, there was a massive brawl. I kept swinging at Aaron and all of a sudden, I hit the ground. His brother joined in the fight as he ran from the bench and hit me in the temple. Their dad came down from the stands and they separated us. As I looked around the crowd, everyone was in shock. I saw many people with the infamous "Home Alone" look on their faces. The fight was long overdue, there was so much built-up tension between us all. The game was canceled, and we were sent home. I felt alone and confused. I never had any parental vision at the game to protect me. I didn't have a basketball dad to watch my every move and to protect me from guys like Mr. Harrison. I dealt with all of this adversity as a 17-year-old kid. Once my adrenaline slowed down, I realized what had taken place and the impact it was going to have on my career. In the game of basketball, perception is everything. Never make decisions based on emotions. I made a decision that night I would regret forever.

I sped home in a state of confusion. *What did I just do? How would this affect me?* I received so many messages and calls but I couldn't answer. When I walked into my house my mom knew something was wrong, she told me to relax and lay down. I fell asleep in her arms, the first time she had any affection from me in seventeen years, but I was shaken. I woke up a couple of hours later thinking it was a bad dream until I saw a call from Coach Brownson. Before I left, I saw him crying. I knew he was disappointed by me, by us, but I was too stubborn to see that. He said that we would be suspended for three days and then we would be allowed back on campus. As for basketball, he didn't know what the next step was, he waited to hear from the district. Those were the longest three days of my life. I received numerous amounts of texts about how the video of the fight went viral and there were even teachers at school watching it. I messaged Andrew, although he got a good hit on me, I knew he was just protecting his brother. I told him, I hoped they were both alright and I apologized. He said the same back and it was over. That's how real men reacted to situations like that. The altercation was a spur of the moment, we didn't hold grudges.

Three days eventually passed, and I was finally allowed back on campus. I received cold stares from the students like I was a convicted felon. I saw Aaron and Andrew as soon as I walked in. We shook hands and went on about our day. The physical part had been fixed, it was the media part that was the issue. The fight had gone viral. If it was just me and a random guy, I'm sure it would have turned heads but nothing like fighting two players that were potential NBA prospects. They were a big deal and I didn't give them enough credit but when I saw how much attention the fight gained, their political stature became apparent. There were forums where people were defending me with anonymous names and people who did the same for them. I called my Iowa State coaches but they blew off the situation. They had guys with much bigger issues. They knew what type of kid I was, and they never second-guessed it.

Later that evening we returned to the school with our parents and had a meeting with the district. We sat in a room with one guy who had to decide if we were going to play the remainder of the season or not. My mom showed up at the meeting and so did Mr. Harrison. Although Mr. Harrison was reserved, my mom spoke up. She expressed that kids shouldn't have to deal with what I was dealing with. Yelling and belittling from another parent should never be allowed she argued. As she was defending me, her voice was breaking up and her arm was shaking. She was scared and intimidated in a room full of men. As she was talking, I grabbed her hand to let her know I was with her during that moment. Although my mom did not attend many of my games, because she said the intensity of basketball gave her anxiety, she was my number one fan. Whenever I would complain or get upset about not getting the results I wanted during a game, she would tell me to quit. She wanted me to be happy and stress-free. She didn't care about basketball and the politics that came along with it. The district official told us we would be suspended one game and if we ended up winning and advancing, only then would we be allowed to return. I never held any grudge against Mr. Harrison, he was essentially preparing me for my future. He was preparing me for what it would be like to play at a high-level and battle scrutiny. He was preparing me for what it would be like to be a black man in America.

I was very mature for my age, I understood why he acted how he did. He had two of the most talented kids in the world at the time and he just wanted to make sure they reached their full potential. I'm sure looking back, there are some things he would do differently but that's what life is about- learning from the mistakes we make. The twins were both great kids and great basketball players. We were very young and made decisions we weren't proud of. We grew closer after that, well kind of.

We were suspended for the first playoff game by the district. Playoffs were single elimination and we needed to win for the three of us to see the court again. I went to the first game we weren't allowed to play in. I rode with a friend and tried to hide, but that didn't go very well. Immediately people pointed me out. I heard whispers and saw pointing fingers. I was embarrassed but I wasn't there for me, I was there for the team. The game went down to the wire and guys stepped up who normally didn't. Well, guys stepped up who normally didn't have the opportunity. We had a very talented team, it was hard for guys to showcase how good they were due to all the talent. We ended up winning, the players kept looking at me during the game for validation and I just wanted to be there for them. It was a brotherhood.

We won and advanced to the next round and I'm sure the team we were going to play next hoped that we wouldn't have won because they knew the twins and I would be returning. No high school team wanted to get matched up with us. We ended up winning the following game, but unfortunately, lost the game after that. The game left everyone speechless. We lost to a team we had already beaten twice earlier that year. A team from our own district, the Hightower Hurricanes. No matter how talented a team is, if there is no comradery and cohesiveness, there is no team, and consequently expectations won't be met. We ended up losing that game, just one game away from the state championship. A team with more than enough talent to win state, but the fight had put guys on different paths. I believe some guys were over the season after the altercation. I felt for the guys that worked just as hard as we did, showed up for every practice and game but never received any recognition. The majority of those guys would never see another organized practice or game. They would never watch film or ride on a yellow bus again, things that we often took for granted. This for most of them was the last basketball game. I wish we could have given them a better experience.

After the big fight with the twins, things started spiraling out of control for our team. News came out that one of our coaches was having an inappropriate relationship with a girl from another high school. Not a teacher but a student, that was frowned upon. Around the same time, we found out that the cheerleaders from our school went on a school sponsored trip and stole alcohol. I was dating a cheerleader at the time, and because of their actions, the cheerleaders were all sent to alternative school. Alternative school is where students were sent with behavioral issues, often times this was male minorites. I am sure guys at the alternative were excited about the new transfers that arrived at the end of that school year. I understood mistakes, but I thought that my girlfriend would have learned her lesson considering she went to jail for stealing earlier that year with another girl whose parents were millionaires. The motive actually made no sense. That's what bothered me the most about kids of privilege. As a minority, specifically a black kid, I understood that I couldn't mess up. If I did, I probably wouldn't have another chance. With all of those events occurring chronologically and the fight being the first. People legitimately forgot that it happened. Well, people from Travis.

CHAPTER 10
AFTERMATH

It took a couple of days for the feelings to settle in; I would never have another high school practice and I would never put on another Travis jersey again. I had spent the last four years there. I was the only player in Travis' history to play on the varsity team all four years. That school was a part of me, but it was time for me to look ahead and concentrate on my next move.

During the season Iowa State signed four transfers under Fred Hoiberg. Two players from Michigan State, one from Penn State and a household name in Royce White from Minnesota. *Where did I fit in all this?* I wondered. I didn't, I don't believe they had any intentions of playing me my freshman year. Now that the season was over, I messaged Fred right away and I asked him where I fit in the equation considering he brought four transfers that only had a year left. He replied and gave me a very vague answer. I asked him a couple weeks later and he failed to respond. I was looking for some sort of assurance from him, but realistically, he couldn't give me that. He didn't know who was going to start or play. He didn't know if someone was going to get hurt or sick. And he definitely didn't know if my game would translate to the next level. There was much unknown from a coach's perspective, and I knew that. But I decided to make yet another decision based on emotions and I started to look at transferring.

That decision was risky, leaving one school and not knowing whether another school would offer me a scholarship. I definitely knew if I left, I would have options. What was unknown was the caliber of the schools and that was important to me. I needed some type of assurance, some type of guarantee. I pondered for days for a solution, and it finally hit me. I asked Chris Gaston to call a school on my behalf. When Chris called, his conversation went something like, 'If Anthony Odunsi were to leave Iowa State, do you guys have room on your team for him?' We went with the indirect question approach because I was a firm believer that you don't leave something until you have another solid in place. If I could get Colorado State to agree, then if I had nothing else, I could rely on them. They had an open scholarship left, I was contemplating getting out of my letter of intent to a school much more prestigious than theirs, and they agreed. They didn't want me to sign immediately as it would look planned and they asked me to wait a week. That was a week too long.

When a player decommits or gets out of a letter of intent, the player is then at the coach's disposal. If the situation isn't handled well, the coaching staff could essentially sabotage a player's future. Coaches are allowed to put whatever transfer restrictions they want on a player. For example, if a player was signed to a Big East School and he wanted to transfer it would be up to the coaching staff to put restrictions on where the player could or couldn't go. Most of the time, the coaches would restrict players from going to another school in their conference. In this situation, the coaches would restrict the player from going to another Big East school. Every once in a while, there were cases that weren't handled the right way either by the coaches or the player, but the coaches had leverage and power so they could restrict the player from playing at a high-level or even the Division I level. Consequently, if Coach Fred wanted to, he could have stopped me from going to another Division I school. The thought of it gave me anxiety but I made another decision based on my emotions. I was furious that he had recruited over me, I thought I was "his guy"; his first recruit, his starting point guard. Fred Hoiberg was trying to keep his job and feed his family, but I didn't understand that initially, I was being simple-minded.

I leaped and got released from my letter of intent to Iowa State. There wasn't much hesitation from them. They asked me if I was sure and then gave me a week to think about it. I questioned how interested they were to begin with. They are a Big 12 school, and I was easily replaceable, but I was too stubborn to see that. They could choose a kid from anywhere, if not me then someone else. I made my decision on a Wednesday. On Thursday, I panicked after going a full day without receiving any calls. I assumed my reputation was hindered by the fight with the twins. Surprisingly, by Friday there were over 10-15 college coaches in the gym. Coach Brownson set it up to where everyone could come on one day and watch me play. The gym was filled with schools from all over the country. We played for about an hour and then I spoke with every coach briefly.

Coach called me later that night and said another school called him that I might be interested in. They fit my academic requirements along with an exceptional basketball program. The call was from Brad

Stephens. Brad had recently become one of the most talked-about coaches in college basketball and was the head coach at Butler University a team from a mid-major conference who had consistently played in the NCAA tournament, Sweet 16 or the Elite Eight the past three seasons in a row. Some coaches won because they had talented players while some coaches like Brad were successful because of their IQ and strategy. He turned mid-major players into NBA players. At institutes like Butler, they required students to be more than just basketball players. They wanted good students and good people first. This was definitely a top contender for me.

It was now April and the end of the academic year was quickly approaching. I needed to make a list of schools I wanted to visit to make a decision. It was difficult as these coaches were like used car salesmen all of whom were selling their schools and basketball programs. I scheduled three visits, one for each of the next three weekends. I asked Coach Brownson to come along with me. We squashed the situation with the fight and rekindled our father-son relationship. I never asked, but if I had to guess, this was going to be his first visit. I valued his opinion, plus I wanted him to get that experience most high school coaches did not have by visiting different campuses, programs, and arenas.

Every college visit consisted of the same set of activities. Some had better-recruiting tactics than others, some offered money, some offered women, and some did things the right way but one thing remained the same, there was no bad visit. Upon arrival to the prospective city a player would be picked up by one of the coaches, typically the one who recruited him, this was usually in the early afternoon to have the rest of the day available. There would be an itinerary for the recruit, so they knew where to be at all times. The coach would either let the player go to his hotel and freshen-up or start the visit immediately. Once taken to the campus, the player would talk to the head coach and then tour the campus. If the campus was small, everyone would walk around and tour the school and for the larger campuses, most coaches used golf carts. They would show you as much of the campus as they could; classrooms, sports facilities, cafeterias, and dorm rooms/apartments. Once that was over the coach would take the player back to the hotel and let him rest up before dinner. Dinner included the company of all the coaches and some players to lighten the mood. After dinner, the coaches would allow the players and the recruit to enjoy the rest of the night, whatever that consisted of. The following day was what I call decision day. The coaches would set a time for players and the recruit to scrimmage. Players felt the pressure to perform but in reality, it was not designed for the high school player to dominate the college players. After the open run, the recruit would have a meeting with the head coach. The coach would give an offer, hoping for the player to commit. Rarely would the coach ask a player to come on an official visit to not propose an offer. That would be a waste of time and resources. After, the player would go to eat with the coach that recruited him and head back to the airport.

We headed out to Fort Collins, Colorado together. Throughout the visit, Coach Brownson never made any comments about what he liked or disliked, and I respected him for that. I don't think he wanted to have that big of an influence over my decision. He came and observed and was there for my support. Considering our agreement, the coaches expected me to pull the trigger and sign. I told them I wanted to be respectful and go on the other visits but I still planned to sign with them. At that exact moment, I had no intention to sign with them anymore. I was never satisfied; I always wanted what I thought was the next best thing. This showed up in every area of my life. If there was a girl I was with but a prettier one was interested, I would want the prettier one. I did the same thing with basketball. I had a school that was fully interested in me, but other schools called, and I lost interest. Coaches did it to players all the time. They would express to a player how interested they were but if someone more talented was ready to sign, they would go with them. It was a shady business.

Coach Brownson and I flew home Saturday afternoon. There was no time to rest, the assistant coach from Butler was flying down to see me on Sunday. Since the coaches from Butler never saw me play, there was only "interest" with no actual offer. The coach was flying down to make sure I fit the criteria of what they wanted out of a player before having me fly out there, this was a part of the recruitment process. Straight from the airport, my assistant coach from Travis, Coach Brett Nixon walked me through the drills we were going to do the following afternoon. He wanted me to be well prepared. The next day the Butler coach came to my high school. I was exhausted but this was a typical schedule for me. If I wanted to be great, I had to keep going, rest was for the weary. After working out for an hour with no air conditioning, I still found a way to exceed his expectations. The assistant relayed the message back to Brad and we set a date to attend Butler University. Butler was an iconic school, with an admirable coach. Coach Brownson agreed to come on the next visit with me also, I knew there was no way he was going to miss it.

During the week coach called me and said there was a problem. The academic requirements to get accepted into Iowa State and most other schools weren't the same to get into Butler. Butler was a private and prestigious university. There was only one logical option to meet their acceptance requirements and that was to retake my SAT while on my visit. For the next couple of nights after school, I prepared, reviewed and studied with the expectations of retaking the test. On Friday while we were at the airport Brad called my coach and told him he got the test waived for me. This was a huge relief; the SAT wasn't something a kid could study for in a couple of days, but I had planned to do my best anyways. I was stoked to visit a program that had such a winning culture.

We had our itinerary set for the visit. Upon arrival we went out to eat, toured the campus, and then I went back to the apartments to hang out with the players. I was hosted by Shelvin Mack, he had a great stint in the NCAA tournament, but it was said that he would be going to the NBA the next season. If he left, it would be great for me but bad for the program. I wanted him to leave because that would open up an opportunity for me to play right away. That's the way my mind worked, I wanted instant gratification. I never thought about sitting out a year or two to develop in college. I wanted to play right away, I felt I was good enough and I wasn't going to settle for less. After hanging out with some of the players, the assistant coach picked me up. On our way home I said something that would affect Brad's perception of me. I asked the assistant coach what I needed to do to start, and that I did not think the guard they had there was better than me. The guard I wanted to replace was named Ronald Nored, he was also the player closest to Brad. The assistant coach gave me a simple and short response, but I am almost certain he called Brad after he dropped me off and explained the conversation we had.

The next day I could feel the mood change. According to the

itinerary, I was supposed to have a one-on-one meeting with Brad. It never happened. I knew where I'd messed up. Brad didn't want egotistical players. He was a coach that prided himself on the team, comradery, culture, and hard work. He didn't want to coach kids who were only worried about themselves. I never got that one-on-one meeting with Brad nor did I get that offer. I learned from my mistake; one word or sentence can cost you everything. When I was leaving, he said he would think about what he wanted to do, whether he wanted to offer or not, but he had his mind made up. When I landed Brownson called and delivered the bad news, but he didn't say anything that I didn't already know. I learned a very valuable lesson that day. I hated the circumstances that it happened under, but I was appreciative of the lesson learned.

After a couple of days, I received a call from a reporter inquiring about my updates on schools and where I thought I was going to end-up. I had failed to mention Colorado State on my list of schools and immediately they contacted Brownson. It was an honest mistake, but I also wasn't interested anymore. The process had begun to wear on me. It had started to become the most frustrating part of my life, I just wanted to be a kid. I just wanted to enjoy the rest of my senior year. If I didn't make a decision soon, I would end-up missing my senior prom.

Chris Gaston called me in the middle of the night, I knew it had to be important because he never called me at that time. He said a coach from the University of Utah messaged him and asked if I was available. 'Utah? What conference is that in?' I asked. I was so self-centered that all I was worried about was the prestige of the university, rather than being somewhere that best suited my goals. Players had to be careful about the schools that came in the last minute. At times, the college recruiting process was trial and error. Schools would bring in a group of guys knowing that half would transfer out the following year. Some schools brought as much talent in as they could without thinking about the player's best interest. This started to become my narrative, schools pursued me because I was one of the best players still available. They didn't follow my season or know the ins and outs of my game. They looked on a list where I was ranked 151st in the nation and previously signed to Iowa State and decided to make me an offer because of that.

The University of Utah had just switched conferences and made a coaching change. They moved into the Pac 12, which was arguably the best conference in the country to travel on top of being a Power Five Conference. Utah played all the California schools; Cal Berkeley, Stanford, UCLA, USC, and a couple of other spots on the west coast that were monumental. It's always good to be a part of new staff with coaches that want you to succeed over the other players that were there from the previous coach. I flew up to Salt Lake City, Utah, but this time by myself. When I arrived, the entire coaching staff was there waiting with Utah gear from head to toe and I met Head Coach Larry Krystkowiak, he was about 6'10" – a big guy. He was the first head coach that personally came to the airport for me. Typically, head coaches were a little too "Hollywood" for that but I believe Larry wanted me, so he made a little more effort and I appreciated that.

I didn't meet any of the players because school was closed for their summer break. Although I didn't go to any parties or attend a football game like the other schools, I still liked Utah. They had mountains and a scenery that set them apart from any place I had ever seen. Salt Lake is a reserved city, somewhere I could see myself starting a family. One piece of advice someone told me was to pick a school you would want to go to if basketball was non-existent. In case I was hurt, or I didn't play, I needed to be somewhere I enjoyed. Utah was also a big school, part of the Bowl Championship School (BCS) Power Five schools. Larry assured me that I would play because there weren't enough players on the team and I jumped on the opportunity. It's interesting because all these schools offered different things, some more than others, but playing time was the most important to me, that's the main reason I was there. I didn't have my one on one with Brad but I got it with Larry. He talked to me about his time in the NBA and his workout with Michael Jordan. I was to naive to understand that he probably told that story to every recruit he had. I thought I was special, but it was warranted because up until that point I had a lot of success in my life.

I ended up committing to Utah before I left town, another decision based on emotions. Instead of consulting with my mom, Coach Brownson, or any one of my mentors I went with my gut. The summer school was about a month away, but I didn't even think about it. I just wanted to get back and attend my prom and enjoy the rest of my senior year and enjoy being a kid. I had become one of the most popular names down south as every one of my visits was documented. I finally signed, and I was finally free. I knew I was making a rushed decision, but I didn't care, it felt right.

I always talked about how ready I was for college and how I was over high school. This was common terminology when most endured four years of high school. I would soon learn patience and learn to enjoy the moment. This was the last time I played basketball for fun, the last time that life wasn't so serious. After prom came final exams, and then graduation. Graduation and getting a high school diploma was a big deal. Travis High tried to make sure no one fell short of this achievement. A week after graduation I was due to report to Utah for summer school. It was bittersweet. I left friendships, family, and a high school legacy. I would have to restart and try to reinvent myself in Utah. The moment I stepped foot on a college campus everything changed.

CHAPTER 11
UTAH

They scheduled all incoming players to arrive in Salt Lake around the same time, so we took a massive bus back to campus. The first encounter wasn't awkward, rather more intimidating; we were all there to do the same thing. The majority of the team was new. I researched all the guys and looked up their basketball stats before my arrival. This consisted of the birthplace, a summer AAU team, rankings, and most importantly other college offers. A lot of the information was irrelevant, but the offers were an indication of the caliber of the individual. I am certain I wasn't the only one guilty of this.

They brought us in on a Friday and let us acclimate to our accommodation. We were all assigned to a unit that consisted of four bedrooms and two baths. We were dropped off and expected to figure everything else out. Although we were meant to get along with everyone, there was still a sense of competition. On Sunday, we had our first team meeting and on Monday we were set to begin classes. During the team meeting, everyone introduced themselves including their names, where they were from, and what they wanted to bring to the team. There was another guy from Houston on the team and we never spoke, he didn't want anything to do with me. I knew exactly what type of atmosphere they had the year prior when two people from the same hometown didn't speak. It was a competition and some guys weren't out to make friends. None of the coaches acted how they did on their visit. They weren't as welcoming. I quickly knew that every decision I made that year would affect me when it came time to play. In the meeting were all the players including scholarship and walk-ons. All of our coaches and staff including video coordinators and managers, the health trainer, weight lifting instructor, and our academic advisor were there as well. It was a complete 360 degrees from what I was used to and to be honest I was overwhelmed, all the freshman seemed to be.

I understood early how important junior college guys were. Junior college or JUCO was an opportunity for players who didn't have the grades or weren't recruited to reinvent themselves. It essentially gave guys more time to mature. Most did two years in junior college and they added immediate experience and maturity to a college program as a junior. They were more mature and had already been in that situation before.

The staff introduced themselves and spoke a little bit about what their role was on the team. Everyone's phone number was presented on the sheet and we all had to meet with the academic advisor one by one to discuss classes and location. We chose our major months before arrival but for freshmen, it did not matter. They put the freshmen in the same easy classes so we could get the hang of things. Although we all had different majors, there were still core classes and electives that everyone had to take. You would think that all the freshmen would stick together but it was the exact opposite. Everyone was so focused on themselves that none of us built a rapport.

The summer was easy, they set it up that way. We only took two classes and attended them four times a week for about an hour each class. We were only allowed per NCAA to work out as a team twice a week, so there was a lot of free time. We ate, went to class, and slept a lot. The other freshmen and I lived in the gym that summer, I think we knew we had a lot to prove. But the older guys would never come to anything but team stuff. I saw this as an opportunity to take their spot. If they didn't want to get better, then I would catch or surpass them. The coaches weren't around much, they were out recruiting during the summer. Sometimes they would all be there for team practice but most of the time it would be one coach running it. Every coach had their favorites. A lot depended on who recruited you to come in. My coach was DeMarlo Slocum, he was on the Colorado State staff and left before I went on my visit there. He would always show me favoritism by messaging me after practices to keep my spirit high and calling me out during workouts. I was told at a young age if your coach yells at you he cares but if your coach never says anything to you it means he's not concerned. The summer school went on for about eight weeks. I flew home for about two weeks and then I had to report back for the actual school year.

My mom decided to come with me to help me get settled in before the school year started. The summer school semester was so short, I didn't even buy a television. I used my computer for entertainment but for the school year, my mom wanted me to be well prepared. She was so proud to have a kid traveling around playing basketball. She had made so many sacrifices for me, I was grateful that I could save her the expense of college by landing a full scholarship. After we arrived in Salt Lake City, I immediately headed to campus to check in on my housing and pick up my room keys. I was so thankful my mom came and helped me move in, it wasn't like the summer, I would need so much more for the school year.

We looked over my room for what I needed and headed to Walmart to purchase the essentials, everything from deodorant to blankets, hangers, and towels. My mother made sure I didn't lack anything. Right before we walked out of the store, she told me, 'Go get protection,' in my head I thought, *Mom it's Utah, you don't need a gun.* Then she said, 'Do you know your size?' And right then I threw up in my mouth. We never spoke about sex but we didn't have to. That day my mom and I got closer in the weirdest way.

We left the store and headed back to set up my items in the room. After we grabbed a bite to eat, I showed my mom around campus. She wanted to hang out that night, but I received a text from my teammate saying there was a party later. The summer was so boring because no one was around, I was intrigued to see how the party life in Utah would be. I had become quite infatuated with the nightlife ever since prom. I never engaged in any parties or anything in high school so I partook in college.

I left my mom at the hotel and dressed for the party. I had grown close to a basketball player on the women's team. She was attracted to women and that worked out so good for me. She was my wing woman. I hung around her more than my teammates. We were so close that one time during the summer school she walked out of practice and the coaches asked me if I could talk to her. We went everywhere together, we were joint by the hip.

The party was great, it included all of Utah's athletes from the softball, basketball, ski, and swimming teams. There were so many women, I didn't know what to do. College was unique, especially one of that size. Utah had over 40,000 students, with double the number of women than men. You could do things, and no one would know unless you told them, it wasn't small like high school. I did a lot of things with a lot of different people and never told anyone.

Just like summer, we had a beginning of term meeting. It would cover the same basis as the other meeting we had but with more emphasis. Instead of practicing two times a week, we had a variation of team practices and individuals. I looked at the schedule and I didn't know how I would have time to even call my mom. From 7 am until about 9 pm we would be busy every day. A typical day included a team lift from 7 am to 9 am. These weren't easy lifts either, added to three days of weights and two days of intense conditioning. From 10 am until about 2 pm everyone had class. The class times depended on your major. We then had practice from 3 pm to 6 pm, and study hall from 7 pm to 9 pm. The training table was right after but most of us took our food to go. Training table was a spread of food we received after practice. It was always high- end, some type of steak or sea food. Study hall was a time allotted for us to complete our homework. Our homework was submitted to the academic advisor first and then submitted to our teacher. He would review and give it back with any corrections. There were times I would submit a paper to the academic advisor and I would get a completely different paper back. This was the program's way of making sure players didn't fail. He was our insurance; some utilized the advisor, but most didn't. Academics was important to me, I never lost sight of what could happen if I became injured. Education mattered and I did everything I could to make sure if basketball was to end, I would have a fallback plan.

Playing Division I basketball at that level was different. The rigorous schedule took a toll on me. At times I would be studying and then wake-up the next morning in the same seated position. The basketball program was paying for my education, they sure got every dime out of me, they worked me to full capacity. That schedule continued the entire year.

As the season approached, we had a team get together right before Midnight Madness. Midnight Madness is an annual event celebrating the upcoming season in which a team opens their first official practice to the public, often combining it with a pep rally and other fan-friendly activities. The night before we went to coach Krystkowiak's house, ate, and relaxed. Coach played in the NBA and he was also getting millions for coaching us. It translated because he had one of the biggest houses I had ever seen. It even had a playground slide indoor for his kids. He was a family man. He always had one of his kids with him at workouts, practices, or any team event. I had a lot of respect for him because of that. I wished days like that would never end. Coaches took basketball so seriously at the collegiate level. It wasn't for fun anymore, it was a business.

The next day they split us up into two different teams for Midnight Madness. The coaches did a decent job splitting us up, the teams were equal in talent. Our game didn't start at midnight like most Universities, it was Utah. They had a lot of religious restrictions, so we started around eight that night. The best part about the game was everyone had a chance to play and showcase their abilities. I played well, I also knew the plays and used that to my benefit. Consequently, I got a bunch of steals, had some points, and assists. It was surreal, I was finally in the Pac 12, one of the most iconic conferences in college basketball. Every time I scored my face popped up on the jumbotron. I did everything I said I was going to do and now I just had to find a way to get into the NBA. After the game, we signed autographs for hours. It was a night I would never forget and a night that I would hold onto because there weren't many more nights like that.

The following day, we were at a tailgate and I received an article titled, "Odunsi brings promise." I sent it to everyone back home. The article talked about how I played well during the scrimmage and my bright future in Utah. I held my head high with confidence over the next month in preparation.

Our best player was an overweight 5'9" guard named Joshua Watkins. Josh was one of the three guys the coaches kept from the previous year and he was a starter. I never saw Josh because he never participated in any of the team activities. He wasn't an arrogant player like Ray, he was just flat out lazy. Our coach called him the "pick and roll demon." When the ball was in his hand, he could make magic happen. When we would run miles, Josh would come in last. When we would do individual workouts, Josh would go half speed. He wouldn't attend weights nor study hall and he repeatedly got in trouble for this. They punished him, made him do two times the workload but he still didn't show up for most team events, I never understood his motive.

I was one of the most athletic freshmen, if not the most athletic.

Although I couldn't jump very high, I was fast, strong, and only had four percent body fat. Yes, at that level they measured that too. I would come first in all sprints, I made sure I was on time and was respectful. I did everything to make sure I got playing time until Josh gave me a little insight into how the system worked. One morning we got a text from the coach to meet on the football field at 7 am instead of the weight room. I knew nothing good could come from this, so I prepared myself. It was early November and it was freezing in Utah. We all rushed down to the field and he explained to us that we were running because someone stole food from one of the cafeteria lines. We all had cards full of money to get whatever we wanted, so this didn't make any sense. No one said anything, we all looked around in confusion. Coach lined us up and we ran sprints called Gassers from one end to the sideline to the other for two hours. Guys yelled and screamed at each other, trying to figure out who was the thief. One kid even started bleeding from the nose because it was so cold. One by one teammates started coming forth, admitting to stealing just to stop the running.

I came in first in almost every sprint and afterward Josh came up to me and said the most powerful words that I would take with me for the rest of my collegiate career. 'They didn't sign you to be a track runner, the most important thing is to make sure you put that ball in the hole. Nothing else really matters,' he said, and he was right. Although Josh showed up late and didn't go hard in anything, he still started in all of our in-practice scrimmages, simply because he could "put the ball in a hole." These coaches were trying to keep their job and continue to feed their families, and I needed to understand how the system worked. I thought that because I made good grades or had the big schools recruiting me and I was nationally ranked, I would start. The reality is once you step foot on campus, the politics end. Players had about two months to show the coaches their worth, it was complete and unnecessary pressure.

A new environment can often lead to adversity. Due to a new setting, there is a lack of familiarity and comfortability. It was hard being eighteen and attending school in a different state. A state where they had different beliefs, ethics, morals, and religion, along with having a very minute percent of the African-American race. I was given a basketball scholarship, I didn't have to write an entrance exam, pay tuition, or apply to schools, they came after me. Instead of complaining, I tried to be thankful. Things started to change quickly, as the season was quickly approaching. The coaches knew who they wanted to play, and I could tell they had their minds made up. During practice, I would notice certain guys they played together. They wanted to see who played well and who they played well with. At times I was in those groups and at times I wasn't. There was an adjustment period for me, but I continued to persevere. We had a couple of practice scrimmages before the actual games started. I didn't start in either of the scrimmages and in one scrimmage the coach forgot to play me the entire first half. This wasn't high school, I couldn't sit at the end of the bench and expect my name to be called. I also knew if I could be overlooked I was not a part of their plans. Even still, I never gave-up, it wasn't a part of my DNA.

On the morning of November the 15th our team had a flight to Boise, Idaho. We were going to play our first game in the next twenty-four hours and I had anxiety all week leading up to the game. A typical travel day was long and exhausting. When we arrived at the bus early morning before heading to the airport, the managers gave us a bag with our name on it with the food we had selected from a menu the night before. We arrived at the airport and our luggage was dropped off by the managers as we headed straight to the departure gate. When we arrived, we went to the hotel and our keys and roommates were already situated for us. We were given an itinerary of where to be and when. We got dressed, went to practice, watched the film, and ate – all in about six hours. The next morning was walkthrough. It was the same thing as we did in practice the night before but at a slower speed. We watched the film again and then rested before the game. There was so much emphasis and time put into every game, I couldn't imagine not playing or being a walk-on, without a chance of playing in the game.

It was my first collegiate game, I listened to the "Take Care" album by Drake on our way to the arena. My entire childhood basketball journey flashed before my eyes and I became emotional, it took a lot to get me to that point. Once we got off the bus, the anxiety turned to excitement. Boise wasn't great but they weren't a new team with a new coach like us. We knew the odds were against us.

I started that game and after a couple of trips up and down the court we were already in the fourth quarter. I finished second on the team in scoring that night with 14 points. I was ecstatic after I played so well. My phone blew up with people all over the country that tuned into my first game. Friends and family were so proud, although we were beaten by 20 points, everyone saw promise. There was no time to celebrate my performance, we were beaten and I knew the coach would make adjustments for the next game. Although I played well offensively, I played awful defensively, and I knew coach recognized it.

We flew back to Utah and coach said we would practice right when we got off the plane, and that's exactly what we did. He mixed up the line the next couple of games. Sometimes I started and sometimes I didn't. I thought to myself, *After having a break out first game coach wanted to ruin my opportunity to get to the next level.* I did what I was known for and ran from the situation. I made a decision on emotions and I called Chris Gaston and told him I wanted to transfer. I gave him a list of schools and told him I would go to any one of the schools that were willing to take me. I had no idea on how to overcome adversity, I did what any eighteen-year-old would do. When something didn't go my way, I tried to avoid it and leave. I lacked patience. I didn't want to fight through adversity, I wanted the easy way out. I wanted things given to me. This wasn't AAU or some small situation. Running from this would have consequences. If I were to leave, I would have to sit out a year and I didn't have the stats to prove another school should invest in me. Schools needed players to play right away and when you transfer you must sit out a year, so a coach had to see the player as an investment.

One day after practice, DeMarlo walked up to me and said he heard I wanted to leave. He said that coaches talk, and other college coaches told him I was trying to transfer. He explained that if my head coach found out, he would kick me off or have me playing at a Division II school next year. I denied it and acted as if I didn't know what he was talking about. He even called my roommates to ask if they had heard anything. They told me when questioned they acted cluelessly, however, I didn't listen to anything they said. I didn't have the most reliable teammates, especially the ones I lived with. They were transfers and when we went on the road they would stay on campus. While I was away both of them tried to engage in sexual activities with one of the girls I was dating. There was also the time they left me behind when we were supposed to go to the weight room together. One morning they both were being really quiet and instead of them waiting for me I heard them head off in the car that came to pick all of us up. I had to run four miles to the weight room that day. Consequently, they were unreliable in my eyes.

Eventually, DeMarlo told Larry and he wanted to make an example out of me. Larry and I didn't make eye contact for at least a month and a half after that. There were a couple of times he left me out of drills and inner-squad scrimmages. Another time he made me play defense the entire practice. I fell into a deep depression. I didn't talk to anyone and I didn't go to my classes. It was so bad that in January, during the pinnacle of Utah winter, I slept with my window opened and put my head by the window hoping to make myself sick. I had never experienced such torture, no one had ever taken basketball away from me. I saw everything flash in front of my eyes and I saw my career heading down the drain. For the first half of the season we had practice at 6:30 am, coach always wanted us on the floor an hour before to shoot. Since I hadn't played in seven games, I didn't care about being on time for practice. I walked from my dorm around 6 am. I made the same walk every morning, but this time I was more depressed than usual.

The previous night, cut off my phone and sat in the dark. The tears rolled down my eyes as I felt empty because I couldn't obtain the only thing that made me happy. I couldn't play the sport that I loved. Coaches could take away something a player worked so hard for, I was broken. I started to question my faith and I didn't think God had my best interest. If he did, how could he let me get to this point? Some nights were worse than others, it was tough to know there was nothing I could do to rectify my situation.

On the way to the gym from the dorm was a railroad track, the same one I passed every morning. As I approached the track, I heard a siren from the train coming around the corner. I stood on the tracks and closed my eyes. I felt like I had hit rock bottom and I wanted everything to end. I knew that if I closed my eyes long enough it would. At that moment while my eyes were shut as tightly as they could, I had a visual of my mom and sister and everything we had done for each other. Standing on the tracks in front of that train wouldn't fix my problem and it would just make their lives worse. At that very moment, I quickly jumped out of the way and the train barely missed me. For a second, I stopped hearing sirens, and I got my "wake up call." Life is a lot more valuable than basketball.

When I arrived at practice, I apologized and made some excuses as to why I was late. I started to work hard again, I had an epiphany from that situation. Eventually, the coach started to play me again. Not much but it was better than nothing. I did my best to enjoy the Pac 12 lifestyle. We played iconic teams, we traveled to the nicest states and cities. I was able to experience things guys never would. I changed my perspective. *How dare I be selfish and stay depressed?* I thought. I enjoyed every moment for the rest of that season.

It was the first game in the Pac 12 tournament, and we were one of the lowest seeds, so we had to play one of the top teams, the Colorado Buffaloes. They had a freshman by the name of Spencer Dinwiddie who was going to be a first-round draft pick. I didn't care about any of that. I knew before I ended up transferring, I wanted to prove to Larry I belonged on the team and in that conference. I soaked in everything, I listened to the same Drake song as I did on my way to the first game. After I got my ankles taped and put on my jersey for the last time. I looked around the locker room, took a deep breath, and reminisced on the year. I knew that once this game was over and the buzzer rang, I would never wear a Utah jersey again and everything would change. I got in the game and immediately became effective. The coach had confidence in me, he looked at me and nodded his head and at that moment I knew for the rest of the game I had his trust. The game was televised and people watched from their homes. I didn't know if I would play for a school of this caliber again so I went all in. I scored 12 points in 15 minutes. I belonged in the PAC 12, the coaches knew it and so did I, but once again the decisions I made deviated me from the path of success. The reality is; as a player, you're only as good as your last season. I entered my name in the transfer list for 2012 the following day.

After the season the coaches set up meetings with five guys from the current team. They took them out to eat and explained to them they wouldn't see any time the following year. In other words, they were telling the players they weren't wanted in the most respectable way. They also reiterated that they didn't feel staying another year would be beneficial. Per NCAA rules; coaches can't force players to leave a program. Often times what would happen is the coaches would tell the players they had no future on the team and consequently most players would leave and go somewhere they were wanted. That's exactly what happened, the five players they took out to eat ended-up transferring on their own. They already knew I wanted to leave so there wasn't a discussion.

The coaches tried to make it seem as if they helped players find schools. They were just doing their job. If a coach called and asked about a player, they would tell them the truth and maybe add a few white lies, to help them find a home. As for me, they didn't try to help. Instead, they tried to hurt me and while I'm sure Coach Krystkowiak wasn't aware, DeMarlo never answered any calls from schools that were interested in me. Thankfully, schools still found a way to contact me and they told me that he wouldn't call them back after leaving a message. When DeMarlo spoke to me, he said he didn't receive any calls and didn't know what the problem was. I understood I made him look bad and I didn't hold anything against him.

The schools that reached out to me were schools I had never heard of before and I was too caught up in my ego to play for a "non-power five" school. I decided to go to junior college in hopes of getting back to a high-level. Junior college was an option that players from high school chose if they didn't have the grades or the college offers they wanted. It was also a way for transfers like me to have another chance at getting recruited without having to sit out a year. Of course, I wondered if I chose junior college, what people would say or think. This was an embarrassing move for me, so I deleted all forms of social media and disappeared.

**2011-2012 University of Utah Men's Basketball Team.
Anthony Odunsi (#3)**

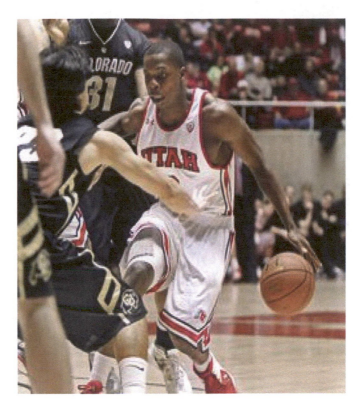

Anthony Odunsi (#3) attacks Colorado defender during PAC 12 League play.

CHAPTER 12
JUCO

Initially only small Division I schools sought after me, but as the school year came to an end and summer approached, more junior colleges contacted me. Attending JUCO wasn't anything I intended on doing, but it did allow me to have the option to choose from a wide range of schools. People called and tried to convince me not to go to JUCO. Some said that it was corrupt while others agreed on the move. One comment was consistent and that was, 'Ant you're not a junior college guy.' I had involved too many people in my decisions, it became detrimental and everyone had an opinion. Eventually, I realized I shouldn't listen to everyone because some didn't have my best interest. I didn't come to that realization until one of my old AAU coaches told me not to commit to a school and that he was going to bring a school from Texas up to Utah to work me out. He claimed that if he could get on staff it would be beneficial for me considering he would always be in my corner. This was my life and people I was close with tried to take advantage. People would put another person's future at risk in order to improve theirs.

I could attend any JUCO in the country, they all wanted college transfers especially one who played in the Pac 12. I had a lot of them contact me, but I only took two seriously, so I visited both. One was a top-five junior college every year called, Indian Hills, which always had players committing to high-level schools. The coach called me one afternoon with the Indiana University head coach on the phone. The Indiana coach praised the junior college and the coach and told me it would be a great stepping stone to get me back to the level I wanted to be at. It was in Iowa and had a reputation of bringing in players with behavior issues. The coach's first question to me was how I would react if a fight was to break out? Immediately this became a deal-breaker, I didn't want to have to endure an atmosphere like that for an entire season. I had just left a traumatizing environment which almost led me to take my life and I wanted my future to be stress-free.

The other option was Tyler Junior College (TJC); it was the same junior college that Jimmy Butler attended. At that point, after all that depression, I wanted to be near family. I asked myself the same question I asked before making my first decision out of high school, "If basketball was to end tomorrow, what school could I see myself at?" This was an important exercise because I did enjoy Utah outside of basketball. Most junior colleges were in rural locations, the thought of being in the middle of nowhere in Iowa if things didn't go as planned didn't sit well with me. I went with my gut and I committed to the school in Texas. The head coach was, Mike Marquis. He was an overweight, short Caucasian, who thought he was funny. In reality, he made everyone uncomfortable. His biggest selling point was, at my size he was going to let me play full-time point guard. At my size, this was hard to do but I knew if I could get a coach to agree, it would take my recruiting to the next level.

Mike assistant Troy Johnson was a friend of a player who I was very close to named, Johnny Bryant. Johnny was a University of Utah ex-player, who worked me out after I transferred. Not only that but he kept my spirits high during the entire situation. He was a great friend and a child of God. We quickly built a rapport before I left the state. After he vouched for the coach and the program, I decided to take a closer look. I wasn't going there to find friends. I was only going to be there for a season, I wanted to find the best situation for me to reinvent myself.

After lacking attention from Larry, I needed assurance and confirmation. Mike seemed like a nice guy. Even after I committed, he continued to message me as if he cared. Recruiting is like trying to date a woman. Initially, a man sees a woman he likes and pursues her. Once he feels he has her, he naturally releases the pressure. It was the same with basketball. Coaches spent a great deal of time recruiting a player, once the player committed, the coach lost interest and started working on the next recruit. I spent the rest of the summer at home excited. I had the opportunity to hang out with friends and family. But I should have seen this as a red flag. Unlike four year Universities, junior colleges didn't have a mandatory summer school and I would soon find out why.

My old AAU teammate Wes Cole decided to drop me off at the campus. On the drive up he did some research about the school. He explained that the year prior, there was a brawl between the men's basketball team and the men's football team. Later, all the players involved were expelled. I had no idea, Mike failed to mention that to me. It made sense because he only had three players returning from the previous year. Out of shock, I told Wes to stop the car. He parked on the side of the road in the middle of nowhere, I cursed repetitively while feeling full of rage. The entire reason I chose the TJC over the Indian Hills was because of the atmosphere. In reality, they were both the same. What did I expect? Multiple people warned me I was not a "JUCO kid." Most kids who attended JUCO lacked grades or had some sort of behavioral issues. At that moment, I got yet another "wake up call." Things aren't always what they appear to be, I should have done more research. Wes and I both knew I didn't have a choice but to go, so he continued driving. I didn't know what I was getting myself into, I soon found out the brawl was the least of my worries.

When we arrived, we both went silent for a second and just stared at the accommodations on campus. The dorm housing looked like a house on a plantation farm. It was solely for the athletes. One hallway was the entire basketball team, the other was soccer. The hallway consisted of seven rooms and in each were two players. Up until that point in my life, I never had a roommate. Mike and I talked before my signing and he said he was going to arrange a room just for me. He had lied again. I knew it was going to be a long year, but I had already signed to the school and I didn't want to be labeled as detrimental to the program.

My dorm room was old and had cement walls, we froze during winter. The sink was in the room, so if one of us needed to brush our teeth, cut our hair or do anything near the sink, the other person had to hear it. The bathroom was disgusting and what made it even worse was I had to share it with two other guys from the other room. Four guys in total using one toilet and one shower. There was a 10 pm curfew and a sign-in sheet for visitation in case anyone had visitors before that. Depending on the time it made women feel very uncomfortable because everyone saw them come in and out. I felt like I was in prison with all the restrictions. I always found ways to finesse the system. If it was late, I instructed my female visitors to dress up as men and wear baggy hoodies and sweats. I would leave my key in a designated spot outside and they would walk in with their hoods as if they lived in the building. For the most part, it worked, then there were a few times when security came and knocked on my door right after. My assistant coach had the worst situation. He was playing house with grown men. Fortunately, he had his own room but he spent most of his time in the hallway chaperoning our every move.

I soon realized that junior colleges weren't funded like universities, especially when it came to athletics. We didn't have an academic advisor, even though we desperately needed one. The assistant coach, Troy Johnson was taking care of all the managerial duties. He was a 40-year-old man with two kids who lived in California and still worked like he was new in the industry. He washed our clothes, cleaned up the locker room, and even taped our ankles before practice. There was no way he was certified to do so, but that was the hand he was dealt. At most schools, there were younger coaches in the assistant coach position who wanted to move up to the university level. I had a lot of respect for Troy. He instilled trust in me, and our relationship grew because of it.

On my first day at campus, I was falsely accused of stealing food. After tasting some of the best cafeteria food I had ever eaten in my life, I decided to go back for seconds. I did what I was used to, I went in, grabbed another plate, and walked out. One of the cafeteria employees saw me and yelled, 'He's stealing, he's stealing.' My teammate ran up and explained to them that it was my first day and I wasn't aware of the rules. I expressed to him that at my last school we had a buffet, and we could go back as many times as we wanted. His response was, 'Welcome to junior college.' The cafeteria closed at 7 pm, so we spent a lot of money on late trips to fast-food restaurants.

For me, it was a major adjustment but for the other players this was normality. They hadn't seen any difference. Although I was spoiled by going to Utah, I never forgot who I was and where I came from. I never let the lack of materialistic amenities interfere with why I was there. Junior college was going to allow me the opportunity to lead a group of guys. I got along with most of my teammates, but on every team, there is always an exception. There was always at least one player who put himself before the team and in this situation, he would be the player closest to the coach. His name was DeAndre Harris and his dad also played for Coach Marquis. I'm sure the coach felt inclined to take care of him in some way. He was the epitome of cancer on a basketball team, but the coach never said anything to him. He never went to class, he never showed up to meetings, he smoked weed and broke curfew. Although he was also talented; I knew he would never reach his potential because there were no four-year schools that would allow him to get away with any of the stuff he was doing. My coach failed to realize that he wasn't helping DeAndre and by not holding him accountable, he was only hurting him. Because of this, the rest of the team was forced to grow close. Late at night, we always picked one room to hang out and talk. I appreciated that about junior college, it was a brotherhood and it was visible when we were on the court.

Before the first official practice, we only played 5 on 5, over and over again. There was no structure and no plays. Mike was a control freak. He picked our seat in the locker room, he also chose our jersey number. The worst part was he made us walk into his office and talk to him every day before a certain time. Some people have power and use it, others have power and abuse it, he was the latter. I didn't want to be in junior college and every conversation I had with him was about where I would play next. I know it was a bit selfish to think like that, but I felt like that situation should have been understood since players strategically went there to leave in a year or two. He started to resent me, and I believe it was our conversations about my future that made him feel this way.

Initially, my social life outside of basketball was nonexistent. I struggled with my identity, I didn't want to go anywhere or talk to anyone aside from my teammates. Since I deleted my social media my relationship with a lot of my friends fell off. The first party I was forced to attend was shot-up and after that, I didn't go to another party for the rest of the year. None of the girls approached me until the season started, but it was always that way. Something about being in the spotlight made me more attractive to women. Before the season started there was a blonde cheerleader that I was attracted to but she was interested in DeAndre. He had tattoos from the neck down and had the "bad boy" aura that girls were infatuated with ironically. After three games, she left him and wanted to date me and I gladly took her in without hesitation. I never thought less of any of the girls I picked up during the season, I understood how attractive someone was in a jersey, especially the best player. I used it to my advantage.

Although I wasn't too particular about Mike, one thing I loved about him was his practices ran for only an hour. He would put sixty minutes on the clock and let it run down without stopping it. If there was something we weren't doing right, he would never stop and correct us, we would just work on it the next day. I wasn't opposed to the hour-long practices, it worked out to my benefit. After, I would take a teammate or two and run through drills. At Utah, I couldn't walk after practice due to the duration and intensity. Having more freedom allowed me to improve during the season. All of the players had respect for me, I was the most talented and I worked the hardest. It gave everyone else a reason to want to get better.

The first practice of the year coach split us up into teams, slammed the ball down, and said, 'Show me who is a starter.' This resulted in absolute chaos. I felt like I was part of a WWE match, there aren't words to describe what I experienced that day. Everyone wanted to show their worth.

On our first game, the coach sent us a text with our itinerary. First on the list was our pre-game meal so everyone headed to the cafeteria. We were served an old hard biscuit, one piece of sausage, and a piece of bacon. I was at a loss for words, I didn't know how we were going to perform with this in our stomach. At Utah, we would have a full buffet before the game. I had to push through, I knew this was only temporary. Pre-season was a joke, we played intramural teams from universities around the area. This wasn't good preparation, I don't believe we gained anything from these games. As a starter, I would barely play because we would beat the teams by a large margin, he would let the reserves play most of the game. The games weren't competitive.

Our first legitimate game came when the conference started. We played another junior college that already had a big man signed to Oklahoma State. The game came down to the wire, but we ended up losing. After the game, Coach Johnson wanted his voice to be heard. Mike never let him speak, so I guess he took this as a moment to say something, and he went around the room and called everyone out. He yelled at us about what we could do better. When he got to me, he said, 'Ant, you need to stop turning the ball over.' I was still digesting that information when I saw Coach Johnson forced into a headlock by DeAndre. The coach said something he didn't like, and he snapped. In awe, we all rushed to break it up. The craziest part to me wasn't that the altercation took place, it was the fact that everyone's response to it was so normal as if it was expected or as if they had seen it happen before.

Most JUCO'S had poor facilities. There were games I would get my ankles taped on a washer in a laundry room or on a bench outside where I could stretch my legs, rather than at a university where a standard training room is required. The meal before the game was awful and the meal after wasn't any better. It was always some sort of fast-food that didn't refuel an athlete's body.

We were a solid team, everyone understood their role, and that's why we beat teams that were more talented than us. Mike lied about most things that he told me before my signing, but he kept his word when it came to basketball. I started and played all my minutes at the point guard position. My entire life I have moved around to different positions because of my height and strength but Mike kept me at full-time point guard the entire year and it helped my recruiting. I had many of the same schools that were recruiting me in high school trying to re-recruit me for a second time. I wasn't having a breakout year, but it was solid. By mid to late season, I figured I probably wasn't going to go high major. Coach Marquis didn't make any calls for me or push my name out there. Everything I had was off the strength of my name from before. The schools that contacted me were schools that didn't typically recruit junior college kids. Junior college players had a negative connotation to them. Since I was already recruited by prestigious institutes, schools made an exception for me. I received interest from North Texas, San Diego, Santa Clara, Cornell, and Pepperdine. Cornell ended up dropping out toward the end and the University of Albany stepped in.

After the season, Mike and I sat down and listed all the schools that offered scholarships and narrowed it down to where I wanted to go. We wrote everything on a whiteboard and immediately started crossing off names. I listed the schools I wanted and for some reason, he kept talking about a school I didn't mention on the board. I reiterated, I didn't want to go to that particular university, but he was persistent about including them in the conversation. It felt a little weird, but I didn't think too much into it. He did the same thing for my other teammates and was able to manipulate their minds, he was controlling and wanted to feel important. I wasn't going to allow him to decide for me.

Time passed and most of those schools stopped calling, texting, or communicating. Even when Albany came to visit, Coach Mike wasn't present. It was like he didn't want me to succeed. I knew that he would eventually run all the schools away by not answering and I would be stuck going to the one he wanted. I took matters into my hand. I talked to a couple of guys who played for Mike previously, and they mentioned how he makes deals with these college programs. They told me about a player who used to play for Mike. He had a bunch of major offers from Power Five schools but somehow, he decided to go to one of the smaller schools with Mike's son Mitch. Ironically, that smaller school was the only school to offer Mitch, he then transferred from there a year after. After hearing the news, I panicked and reached out to schools on my own. From that point on I took care of my recruiting. I thought it was weird how I had eight schools recruiting me hard and they all disappeared out of nowhere. It was going to be my third school in three years, I wanted to make sure that I made the right decision. I got on a flight to the University of Albany in Albany, New York, and went on an official visit.

I arrived in town late that evening and immediately the coaching staff and I went to eat with a couple of the players from the team. They had two guards who were graduating, and they told me they wanted me to fill in one of those roles. Coaches usually don't recruit junior college players to sit on the bench. They are usually brought in for immediate impact. Fifteen minutes into dinner, I could see that all three of the coaches were pretty reserved. The head coach, Will Brown was very quiet and his two assistants tried to overcompensate for that. Dinner ended and they had a concert for me to attend right after. Albany was a party school and that became apparent when kids were at the school function bouncing off the walls. I don't have any recollection of seeing a coherent student the entire night. I knew the coaches would watch us play the following day, so I asked to get dropped off at my hotel early that night. I was one of those kids who took basketball seriously; I made sure nothing got in the way of me performing at my peak. The following day I had an itinerary sent to me via email of what the day would consist of. I toured the campus, met with academic advisors, and played pick-up with the rest of the team. Everything up to that point was very subpar. I looked up the roster and I already knew the players' weaknesses and strengths. Offensively, I did okay. But defensively I shut down the point guard that would be starting there the next year. The green light went off in my head and I knew it was the school I wanted to commit to. Quite frankly, it's all I had.

The coaches talked about my defense up until the time I left campus. They wanted me to come, start, and contribute. They were top two in their conference every year. I knew if we could repeat while I played a vital role on the team, it would open doors for me. I flew back to Texas and three days later I signed my letter of intent. Albany was consistent in my recruiting, Coach Will Brown flew down twice to watch me from New York in the middle of his season. I knew making it to the NCAA tournament was a major accomplishment and scouts liked winners, so I pulled the trigger. I never got congratulations or anything from Mike, I knew something was up and it was unfortunate he couldn't do the right thing for his players' careers. I never talked to Mike Marquis again after that, never a hi or bye. I got my transcripts and left school.

CHAPTER 13
ALBANY

We arrived on campus early summer. I did my homework on all the players, new and old. I knew what they looked like, where they were from, and most importantly their strengths and weaknesses on the court. There were six incoming players, four junior college players, and two freshmen. The summer apartment was awful, we weren't told that we were staying there until a couple of days before we arrived, it was a typical coaching tactic. There were nicer apartments, but we would only be allowed to move into those during the fall. I saw them when I came on my visit and they were beautiful. For the summer accommodation, there were two to a room, I thought it was complete blasphemy that programs thought it was okay to have two grown men sleeping feet away from each other. But I had just endured it for a year, what was a couple more months? The room was very small, it was equivalent to a Harry Potter hostel. It had a twin-size bed on both sides and there was no air conditioning. I don't think I slept through the night once due to the heat. Most apartment buildings had a cooling unit but not in this particular dorm. Because the winters were so cold in New York, they felt they didn't need it. I never complained about it, I had already experienced worse. If there was one positive trait, I had picked up from my year in junior college, it was to be thankful for the little things. Although the basketball workouts were pretty easy, summer school was a struggle and my classes were the culprit. I had taken all of my prerequisite courses in junior college and the only classes left were those I needed for my major. I was enrolled in all my business classes at once and it was intense to say the least. There were a lot of late nights and early mornings.

Athletic programs used summer school as a way for students to become acclimated to campus and build comradery amongst their team. The coaches were hardly around as they were busy recruiting throughout the summer. Although everyone was trying to prove their worth, summer wasn't the time coaches would recognize you. Summer school flew by and I went home for a two-week intermission. While I was home, my mom purchased me a new car and shipped it to Albany a week before I left for school. I wanted to drive it to New York, but she cut that idea off. I wasn't sure if it was her being a concerned mom or if it was a Nigerian thing, but she saw the worst in all situations. It could have even been something as simple as going to the beach. She would say, "Ahhh don't go to the beach, I know someone who drowned there." Shipping my car to Albany was a safer route.

When I arrived for the fall, I was finally allowed to move into the air-conditioned luxurious apartments. It was four bedrooms and two baths, a big and spacious unit. My room was the first to the right. I had my set-up with my PS4, posters, and black light. My black light was what I used at night to set the ambiance when women came over. It was my third school in three years and I grew numb to the relationship idea. I heard Albany was a party school and I was excited. I knew how to balance basketball, partying, and school. I never forgot why I was there and what was most important. In my apartment, there were three other college players, one of whom I roomed with during the summer. We all had spent the last year in junior college, so we were equally hungry to play and make an impact. We were more talented than the guys they had there, but the talent was minute when it came to playing for Will Brown. Every year my understanding of basketball and the college system grew.

After two years, I started to learn how coaches thought and how little pure talent mattered. A coach's trust, understanding of the offense, and ability to play well with others are all things that will overtake talent. We were more talented than the guys they had there but those players who were there previously had the coach's trust and we would figure that out the hard way. Coach Brown recruited a lot of Australians, there were four on the team and he was recruiting more to come in the following year. I'm not sure how it all started, but our best player was an Australian. I assume he found success and rolled with it. The talent level individually was pretty even, no one was far more talented than the other, but I do feel I was individually the most talented player on the team. It came down to trust and that became apparent.

The first month was dedicated to position-based individuals and team practices. The team practices were short, but it was a way for the coach to evaluate who fit in and who didn't. It took me longer than most to pick up the offenses and their schemes. I struggled to know when and where to create, when to pass, and when to score. Time is not on a player's side in such situations, the ones who picked-up the offense the quickest, had the advantages. I was a breakdown one-on-one player, and I didn't do well when the coaches tried to put me in a box. Gilbert Arenas used a quote that I felt represented me well. "Which is scarier, a pit bull on a leash or a pit bull that is free?" I believe I showed flashes of my potential, but I had to show Coach Brown that I was far more superior than the other players in order for him to hand me the keys to the team.

Slowly but surely the coach started to strategically break-up the team into starters and reserves. The starters were all the guys they had the previous year, and the reserves included me and the other new players. It became so competitive, that one of the freshmen ended up transferring halfway through the year because he didn't see himself playing. Consequently, I grew close to the three guys I roomed with, it was like us versus them. Ede was the one cancer you had on a team, but he wasn't as bad as I was used to seeing. He was just someone that a lot of the guys didn't get along with due to his actions. He was the only New York native and ironically, he was a bit more stand-offish than the rest of us. I started to figure out that it wasn't just him, other students I met around campus who were natives of the state were the same way. I grew to understand their culture. Levan, my other roommate, was a unique individual. He was 6'9" and from the Republic of Georgia. He had tattoos from his neck down. He was the first man I saw with a tramp stamp. The nicest guy on the team but the craziest as well. Of the three, I was closest to Anders. He was a 6-foot kid from Denmark. He reminded me of one of my boys back home, we grew close and were almost inseparable. We went everywhere together, and it showed on the court. He looked out for me and I looked out for him. He was slower than a snail, but he could shoot lights out.

Coach Brown saw me as a versatile wing, a player who could play multiple positions. The other coaches saw me as a point guard. I didn't play well without the ball in my hands, so I tried to show him that if he put me at the point guard position, I could help him win. Midnight Madness came around and our first scrimmage/practice was underway. The fans gathered around like they did at all universities all over the country and they got to see what talent coach had brought in that year. He split us up into two different teams without any type of discrimination. Tip-off went up and I dominated the entire game. I thrive in settings where I don't have to think. I was talented enough to just play, other players needed structure, but I was the complete opposite. I even got yelled at by one of the players from the previous year about not running the offense, but truth be told I didn't know it. I hadn't picked up on it quick enough, so I just played off instinct. I was the top scorer on my team. I know all the guys on the team saw how talented I was and I'm sure coach saw it as well, but would he sacrifice team comradery for one player? That was highly doubtful. The next day before the practice I had a meeting with the coaches. Coach Brown said in a very uncharismatic way, 'All the coaches think you will be better at the point guard, so I will put you there for now.' He said it as if they believed it, but he didn't. For the next couple of weeks, I tried to show him that the other coaches were right, and the ball did belong in my hands. I overcompensated to the point where I would pass up shots trying to get others involved. I struggled with my identity on the team at times. It's always tough when your coach sees you differently than how you see yourself. Unfortunately for most players, this was the case.

The first game was nearing, and it was set in stone that I would be part of the reserves. It happened so quickly that I didn't have time to be frustrated. The assistants would always tell me to be patient, that my time would come. One game went by, then two, then three, and I was still playing minimal minutes. I was the 6th/ 7th man, which meant I was one of the first ones that got subbed in, but the coach didn't sub for long. There is a coach's saying, "Give him a breather." It's when the coach would call on a reserve to relieve a starter. Coach Will was literal when he used this gesture. He would sub players in for three to five minutes and put the starters back in. At the end of games, the starters all played 30 plus minutes out of a 40-minute game. He had the guys he trusted and if you wanted to get in any type of rhythm, you needed to be part of them.

It was our fourth game of the season and we were playing the University of Bucknell. We talked all week about switching on ball screens late in the shot clock. When I got in the game, the exact situation occurred (I had that type of luck). I never got touched by the screen, so I stayed with my offensive player, but the big man ended up switching and we were both on one guy. The guard threw it back to the big man and he made a wide-open three. The coach was furious and yelled at the top of his lungs 'That's why he doesn't play, that's why he doesn't fucking play!' while looking at the other coaches. The entire bench was blown away by Will's remark. I knew things didn't look good for me moving forward. He was making an example out of me because all the coaches vouched for me. I knew it was over, so that night I started to look for a way out. But how? I had already transferred once and according to NCAA rules, I couldn't transfer again. I stayed up until 4 am doing research and found out that players could transfer if they had a family member that was sick. I didn't have anyone that was sick, and you couldn't lie because in-depth documentation was needed. I knew I was out of options. Then I ran across this article of this player who was able to transfer because the university didn't honor an injury he had. He was an athlete at UCLA, who then transferred to Georgetown. I knew he may have known some people politically who had connections to make that move possible. Those were different level schools than the school I attended, and I had to respect that. I closed my computer, prayed about it, and went to sleep.

The next day in practice, something happened that changed my life forever. During practice one of the players on the opposing team came down with the ball and I took a charge. As I fell, I hit my head on another player's knee. I fell down for a second and everyone got up and ran over to me. I looked up and everyone was standing over me in shock. As I got up, I heard Coach Brown say, 'Make sure he doesn't have a concussion,' and at that point, it dawned on me. I could use this as leverage to leave. I immediately fell back down, as if I had fainted. Two players picked me up and guided me to the training room. That evening the team went on the road to another game, but I stayed behind. I was ordered by the trainer to sit at home and rest to see if the "concussion" symptoms got better. Initially, I did have a concussion. My head hurt all the time, and I was extremely sensitive to light. After a couple of weeks, I thought it would be best to continue with the story. I kept the secret to myself. I did extensive research and I fit the criteria. My research revealed I could obtain a medical redshirt if I played less than 20 percent of my games, at that point I hadn't played much. I planned to use the concussion injury as a way to get back home. I knew that with my past reputation, one of the Houston universities would offer me a scholarship.

For the next six months, I would go to the doctor weekly and purposely fail the concussion test. The doctor would ask me something and I would act as if I couldn't remember or grimace as if it hurt me to cooperate. The doctor gave me a set of numbers and ask me to recite them backward. I didn't think I could do that even if I didn't hit my head, so that was the easy part. Every time I went in, I knew it provided me with more documentation and more of a claim to get cleared for a medical redshirt. Initially, our head coach showed empathy. He felt bad about the situation but gradually he grew inquisitive and wondered what was taking me so long to get back on the floor. My teammates, especially the ones I lived with became even more quizzical. When they would leave, I would go out. Thursday through Sunday I was out partying.

One night, I came home at around 3 am. I'd lost my key at the bar and I had to bang on the door for one of my teammates to let me in. The next morning my roommates were hanging out in the living room after returning from their shootaround. They asked why I was going out with my concussion. I asked them to sit down on the couch and I explained to them my plan. They didn't like Coach Brown either, none of them got playing time so I knew I could trust them. I told them about all the research I did when I hit my head and how it was an opportunity for me to capitalize and potentially get myself out of this situation. After I explained, they were astonished. For at least five seconds each of them was speechless. Ede spoke and said, 'Do you think you can think of something for me to get out?' We all started laughing and I told them I needed their help. I never attended practice, so I wanted them to talk to the coaches and validate my injury. Telling them only helped me. That day after the game Will messaged me and said that my roommates told him how bad my head was and that he hoped I got better. I thanked him and chose to stay on his good side. I had to continue to make everyone believe so I took a step further. I called and asked my sister for my mom's email and password. I emailed Coach Brown from my mom's email and pretended as if I was her. I explained that she was frightened and that she didn't care about basketball, that she only cared about my safety, and that for Christmas I would come back home and get a second opinion. That was exactly what I did. When Christmas break came around I went home and went to my doctor, I told him about my situation and that I wasn't feeling well. My only thought process through all this was that

I needed as much documentation as possible.

I went back to school and continued with my plan. Days, weeks, and months went by and it was the same routine. Randomly one day in late January my coach popped up to our apartment unannounced. He walked in with my teammates, but they didn't relay the message. Luckily, I was in bed watching basketball. I had one game streaming on the computer and another on television. There were pill bottles from the prescribed medicine the doctor gave me to deal with headaches. As he walked through the entrance door all I heard was, 'Which room is Ant's?' When he saw me, he looked at me with guilt and empathy. I was lucky that I wasn't doing something that would have outed me. The fact that I was at home in that condition bought me a couple more months. I knew once he came unannounced and saw me like that, he would relay the message and Coach Brown would be sold.

The season was coming to an end, but we were favorites to be in the conference championship. We only had a few more practices left before the conference tournament, so I thought it was a good time for me to pass one of the baseline concussion tests. I went into the doctor's office and finally passed. It wasn't out of the blue, I gradually "got better." When I was cleared, Coach Brown immediately wanted me to practice. I was already redshirting, so I knew that his motive was to watch me practice to see if he could utilize me for the following year, but I didn't want to be a part of his program. He was just like the other two coaches, the pitch to get me to come to play for him was a lie and he probably told the same thing to all the other incoming players that year.

After the doctor cleared me, he gave our basketball trainer clearance to start doing physical activities with me. We started slowly and gradually increased our workload every day. I would have to act as if I was tired, but the truth was since December I was going to the gym with my roommates at midnight. We played one-on-one for hours. We did this several times a week, as long as they weren't on the road. One night, two of my other teammates walked in and saw me working out, they looked at me like they had seen a ghost. I didn't have to even say anything, one of them looked at me and said, 'I would do the same thing.' I couldn't let our team trainer become suspicious, so I always acted as if I was tired during workouts. After the conditioning for about a week, our trainer wanted me to try on-court stuff with a ball. I wanted the coach to let me go, I didn't want him to try and keep me on the team the next year so when we started the practice that day, I said I wasn't feeling good and he lost it. Coach Brown yelled and said, 'He's faking, he's fucking faking!' I knew there was no way he could prove it, so I walked off. That night I scheduled a meeting with him and the other coaches for the following morning.

When I walked into his office at 8 am, I told the coaches I probably wasn't going to play basketball anymore and that I didn't feel healthy. And when the year was over, I was going to go back home and figure out which school my family could afford. I explained to them that I was going to just be a normal student and that the injury I had suffered was pretty grueling. I presented this whole conversation with tears in my eyes. How exactly I made that happen is still surprising to me, but I had to make them believe it. Basketball was my love, it was really all I cared about. I knew I was talented, and I wasn't going to let these coaches ruin it for me. Coach agreed to let me go back home after the school year. He explained he would get me my medical redshirt and he wished me the best of luck. Whether or not he believed me was irrelevant. He didn't care about me. With me volunteering to leave he could bring in another recruit. After that talk, I got another "wake up call." I saw just how heartless and ruthless the basketball game was. The coaches only cared about themselves and they would do whatever they had to make sure they excelled. For the remainder of the season, I attended home games and watched games online.

That year was special, we won the conference tournament by two points. Everyone stormed the court and despite not playing, I got to experience winning. With a conference championship win, we received an automatic bid to the NCAA tournament. I wasn't going to miss the most iconic tournament of the year. After six months I went on my first road trip. We had to play in a game called the First Four. It was a game that was played amongst the lowest-seeded teams. Our school was seeded very low, we had to play a "play in match" and if we won that we would be in the NCAA tournament. We won that game and were picked to play the University of Florida Gators. They had home-court advantage because they were a higher-seeded team.

We flew on a private plane to Florida with the basketball team, cheerleaders, band, and the administration. I was blessed to have played in the Pac 12 and experience the luxury of playing on that level, but the NCAA tournament was a different beast. The excitement from the Selection Day Sunday, where you figure out who you are playing, until tip-off is an unbelievable experience. When we landed there was a band playing for us and cameras all over the players. I wasn't playing but it was a great atmosphere to be around. We went to the hotel and prepared for practice. Later, we had time assigned for film. We had made it that far and we were playing the number one seeded team. The coach wasn't going to pressure the players, he let us enjoy the trip; we had responsible guys who knew the limits. Before the game no one drank or smoked, at least as far as I knew. The guys just hung around the pool, or with their friends and family who came out to support.

Game time rolled around quickly. We dressed, packed our game bags, and got on the bus to head to the arena just like any game, but this time the outcome was much more significant. I had on a suit and tie waiting to support my team. I never had a problem with anyone on the team, so cheering wasn't an issue. I wanted all those guys to succeed and they had so far. We gave the University of Florida a good fight but there aren't many, if any, upsets in the first round. Guys were emotional after the game, it was normal. That team had nothing to hang their head about besides the fact that they would never play with that exact group again. The NCAA funded the whole tournament and flew us back the next morning. From the moment we arrived back to the hotel until we took the bus to the airport we partied. Later that night I got a random text to come to a room on the 11th floor. I thought I was going to get lucky, but it was just the band team and they were absolute animals. They did things I had never seen, I never expected them to party like that. We had a good time, between the players, band, and cheerleaders. I did not go to sleep that night, things were out of control. I ended up flying back to Albany phoneless and with the hangover of the century. It felt like someone was sitting on top of my head.

As soon as we walked off that plane, the basketball season was over. I cleaned my locker and never saw Will Brown again; I didn't have to. The other guys in my room had exit meetings the following Monday. This was a meeting between players and staff, and they discussed the future if there was any. Every player who came in that year transferred except one, the rest were forced to leave. In three separate meetings, Coach Brown explained to Ede, Levan, and Anders how he didn't see them contributing and that they were better off somewhere else. He even told Anders he wasn't a Division I player, which wasn't true. Collegiate sports are cut-throat. If they don't feel you are getting the job done, they just let you go or make it so players had no choice but to leave. I dodged a bullet for the second time, but I wasn't sure I was going to be cleared to play the following year. I still had to apply for hardship and that would be challenging. I wasn't sure why the NCAA made the process so difficult. There were players whose careers were ruined because of coaches. The NCAA had so many restrictions on transferring, a lot of players had to play at levels lower than they should have, I was the one percent who was able to deviate from that.

For the last two months of school, I started to get myself back in game shape. I lifted weights and went to the gym twice a day to shoot and do drills. One day, one of the assistants saw me working out and the next day they were at my apartment asking me to stay. The assistants saw my potential, but the head coach never did and they didn't have much influence over the decisions that he made. I didn't have any reservations over any of the coaches nor the program. I just knew I could help but if the coach and I didn't have the same vision, I had to offer my assistance somewhere else. I declined the offer and went back to Houston.

I received my release, and I was able to talk to any school that would be willing to talk to me. At that point, I'd already transferred three times and had fought with my teammates in high school. I think that it was safe to say schools thought I was a problem. At some point, I had to look at myself in the mirror and ask some hard questions. I had attended three schools and at all three places, I didn't fulfill my expectations. I didn't get along with any of the head coaches but with this last and final move. I prayed that it would be different.

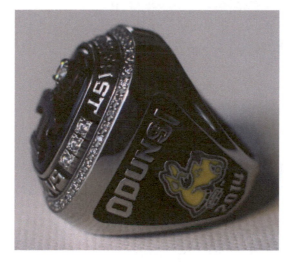

**2013-2014 America East Conference Championship Ring
(Albany Great Danes logo)**

CHAPTER 14
HOUSTON

There are four Division I schools in the Houston area; Texas Southern, The University of Houston, Houston Baptist, and Rice University. I crossed out Texas Southern immediately, their basketball atmosphere was similar to junior college. Ray Penn transferred there and didn't have the greatest things to say about his basketball experience. University of Houston had just hired an NBA coach and he wasn't willing to take a chance on a "washed-up" player from Houston. Essentially that was what I was. Three years into my collegiate career and I had no success on the Division I level. Rice was a prestigious university, if you graduated from there you could land just about any job you wanted, that was my first choice. They were interested and they remembered who I was from high school. I left Albany with a 3.5 GPA so I knew I had the grades to get in. The coach said he would call some guys that were well-known around Houston to do some further investigation. Weeks went by and Rice never responded. Someone decided to speak negatively about my name. I could have treated people differently. I could have talked to people differently. I could have prevented this from happening but yet again I got another "wake up call." I am not sure who they called but I must have had a bad encounter with someone during my young age. As I matured, there were a lot of things I learned over the years. I wasn't mad about the current situation, instead, I learned from it. I didn't have time to point fingers.

I resorted to my second choice, Houston Baptist University (HBU), another school where academics are highly valued. The head coach lived down the street from me, his daughter and I attended the same high school. The only fond memory I had of her was when she walked up to me in the hallway my senior year and said, 'My dad, and I don't think you're good enough to go to the Big 12.'

'So what do you think I'm going to go to a HBU?' I replied.

Despite that bad memory, I found her number and asked her if she could let her dad, Coach Cottrell, know I was transferring back home. At that time I was 21 and I knew how to handle myself professionally. That year HBU had 60 percent of their team transfer including their best player, so it was a great opportunity for me. I just had to convince the coach to take a chance on a player who sat out the entire year due to an injury. Couple of days passed by and I heard nothing from the coach. One afternoon, I received a text from him saying he wanted to talk and hear more about my situation. When he called, he was so amazed at how much I had grown and matured. I wasn't the seventeen-year-old from Travis High who wouldn't talk to anyone but big schools. I was now on my fourth school and every year I became more humble. We had a great talk, we laughed about past times and we talked about the future. He said he had a scholarship available, but he needed to talk to the board to see if they could do the paperwork to get a hardship from the NCAA. He mentioned that he was taking a risk and that potentially there was a chance I wouldn't be able to play. We talked about my injury and how he was hesitant to take a chance on me because of the medical history. I couldn't tell him there was nothing wrong with me. I knew him to always be a coach who prided himself with morals and ethics. If he found out the truth, he wouldn't want anything to do with the situation, so I kept it to myself. If I didn't get cleared, he would scholarship me for two years, but I would play one year of basketball. Honestly, I was lucky he even considered it.

The next day he called to tell me that everyone was on board and we needed to start the paperwork as soon as possible to see if I could get cleared. He set up a meeting with a member from compliance for athletes. Compliance was the department that gathered the documentation from my concussion and passed it on to the NCAA. My case was unique because I didn't return home because someone was sick. So, I thought deeper, I went to the drawing board and pondered about what I could do to solidify the situation. What could I do prevent the NCAA from having doubts about clearing me? I called my mentor Sean Jones for advice. Sean was a former All American defensive end who played for several NFL professional teams. He was also one of the smartest people I knew. I could never get him on the phone but when I needed him, he was there for me. After speaking with him he helped me figure out a way to provide a better case to the NCAA.

I was assigned to a white, very smart guy from compliance. He seemed very knowledgeable about the industry. Immediately, I put my trust in him and reiterated that I wanted to get cleared and it was my last basketball shot. He was the last person on earth who could know the truth about my injury, without a doubt he would stop the entire process. Essentially, the story Sean and I came up with was that my mom fell ill because I got sick in Albany and she couldn't take care of me. She needed to be near me, I needed to come home.

In an email to compliance, I told the representative about my "mother's illness" and how she wasn't well. The entire story fell together. He explained that I made a great case and that I should submit all the paperwork both mine and my mom's to him. I didn't have any paperwork for my mom, but I was relentless. I would do whatever it took, no matter the cost to get cleared to play. I set up an appointment with my doctor without telling my mom. The next day I talked her into coming with me, I told her I needed one last visit to him for my concussion. The truth was the visit was for her. She needed to abide by the story and tell my doctor she wasn't feeling well. My mom went in there and was completely useless. She couldn't believe all that I was doing, but she also wasn't in my situation. I had to get cleared and this was my last chance. I asked her to leave the room, and my doctor and I had a personal talk. That afternoon we left my doctor's office with documentation about my mom's illness. We would just need to come in a couple of more times to show her progress. That's what we did, we came in multiple times as my mom "progressively" got better.

Some days I was optimistic, I felt we put together a great portfolio. Other days, after conversing with compliance I would feel like I had no chance. There were good days and bad days. Often, I would take my frustration out on my teammates. A lot of the guys looked up to me, they knew I played at a level they dreamed about playing at. Instead of mentoring them, I belittled them. I went to summer school, did summer workouts with the team, and put in extra work on the side, not knowing if I would be able to play. Whether I got cleared or not, the coach had to prepare for the season, and I had to respect that.

On September 22, 2014, I got called into coach's office. All three assistants were sitting with a blank look on their face. Coach said, 'Congratulations Anthony, you have been cleared to play this year.' The feeling at that moment was indescribable. From October 2013 to that very day, everything I did was worth it. From the sleepless nights and the phone calls to make sure I was thinking rationally. I was excited, I relayed the message to my family back home and got back to work. This was my fourth school in four years, I was going to make it worth my while. HBU was a small private school consisting of about 3,000 students many of whom had been given scholarships to attend. Whether it was athletic or academic, many of the kids there were given some type of grant to help pay for school. It was conservative, to say the least; a lot of home-schooled kids went there. It was such a small school, that some people who lived in Houston had never heard about it. It was a commuter school so during the weekends, it would be a ghost town on campus. I had already had my fun. It was time to focus, graduate, and concentrate on basketball.

The team's leading scorer the previous season transferred, which opened up an opportunity for me. There were three seniors, two of whom played the same position as I did. The keys to the team weren't handed to me. I tried to take them, and it created a minor conflict in our team chemistry. I was bigger and better, but those players had been with the coach for four years now. I think he felt he owed them loyalty. There was a controversy between the old point guard and me. He was 5'6", there were not many other positions he could play. Coach Cottrell wasn't like some of the other coaches I played for. He cared about the players' feelings and tried to do what was morally right. The other coaches played who would help them win games.

We had a new offense that year and we all struggled with it. It was a good offense, but it wasn't the best offense for our personnel. Coach changed the lineup many times that year trying to figure out which group was most cohesive. One thing remained and it was that I started. Pre-season was a struggle, we played multiple high majors. They are what most people call "money games." A term that is used when a BCS school funds a smaller school to fly in and play at their home court. These schools would always win by large margins and they would always have home-court advantage. The smaller schools would agree due to financial reasons, it also allowed players opportunity to showcase their talent at a higher level.

Due to these money games, I never lacked anything at HBU. I always had new apparel and shoes. We always stayed in nice hotels and ate great before and after games. I wanted to give back, I wanted to help them win. Since HBU was such a small school, everyone knew each other, especially the athletes. Although, I played at two other schools people still knew me as the kid from the Pac 12. I was a fresh face on campus, and I used it to my advantage. I was having an okay season, it started slow as I was trying to figure out the offense. But after a team-high 18 points and almost beating the cross-town rival- the University of Houston, my role on the team changed. I slowly started to become the focal point. With a new offense and new team, it was too hard to put together a great season and we finished around 500, which was better than their previous season, but it wasn't good enough. I finished averaging around 13 points and received honorable mention. I had always heard about the drastic difference players see after staying in a program for multiple years. I transferred every year, I could never really watch myself develop in a system. I would get one more chance and I would have to make it count.

The 2015-2016 year rolled around. We lost three guys but replaced them. Overall, we became a better team. Guys understood their role and I thought we would be a bit more successful than the previous year. My preparation for that year was different than any other. I took Bikram Yoga classes, I dieted, and I went to the gym two to three times a day. I was always a hard worker but I knew this was my last opportunity to prove I could play on the next level. Coach wanted to switch me from the point to the shooting guard position. He wanted me to have the green light and score, and he thought that I was incapable of doing both for some reason. His vision was different than mine and because of that the entire pre-season, coach and I bumped heads. He wanted to start a player at a point who had no experience, nor did he deserve to play. He never went to the gym or took basketball seriously but he had God-given gifts. He was athletic and was by far the best defender on the team. Even still I didn't think that made a case for him to be the starting point guard. The point guard position is the most complex position in basketball. A point guard is the nucleus of the team, the position that holds a team together, like a quarterback. The game slowed down for me. I was seeing and doing things I couldn't do the year before. I finally saw the luxury of growing within a system. I knew the plays, where I was going to get my shots, and when other players would be open. Apart from the new guys I knew my teammates' strengths and weaknesses. I knew what they could do, and I put them in positions to be successful. This all made my job easier as the main ball handler on the team. Instead of listening to the coach, I would just take the ball and run the point.

Over time this caused conflict.

Our first game was in Las Cruces, New Mexico against the New Mexico State Aggies. They had a future NBA player, Pascal Siakam. At that time we knew he was good, and were aware that he would probably go to the NBA. The outcome was pretty bad, and I didn't have my best game. Next was a home game against a Division III school, and we won. It was common practice for the bigger schools to schedule us to gain confidence and add a win to the schedule, we did the same. After that, we played in the Cancun challenge, an all-inclusive tournament, where teams played two games in America and two in Mexico. We lost our first two games, one against Texas Christian University (TCU), and the other to Illinois State University. I had a decent game against TCU, but I had the worst game of the year against Illinois State. I had one game a year where my mind and my body weren't on the same page, Illinois State was that game. I had 7 turnovers; I couldn't get the ball past half court. This trickled over to my next game.

During our first game in Mexico, I only played seven minutes with no points. I saw my career flash before my eyes. We weren't playing well nor were we playing up to our potential. After our first game in Mexico, I messaged the coach and asked if we could talk. We never texted, so it was an awkward situation for me, but it had to be done. He met me in the lobby of the hotel. Coach isn't a confrontational person so when we sat down and talked, he looked the other way. He asked why I asked to meet and explained to me that he thought I was going to ask to indefinitely come off the bench. Contrary to what he thought, I came to ask him *what in the world he was thinking by benching me?* I grabbed his hand, and he opened his eyes really large as if he were in shock. I told him to trust me and from that point on our relationship changed. With the coach's trust, I scored nothing lower than 17 points per game for the remainder of the regular season. I wasn't always the biggest fan of him and I can almost guarantee he wasn't the biggest fan of me but something happened that day and it sparked a special bond between us the rest of the season. I won the All-Tournament team in Mexico and it was the start to a great season for my team and me. The next game was played on our home court versus Rice University another Houston team. They were the team that passed on me two years prior when I tried to transfer. I knew I had to make a statement. Anytime two in town teams played it was a big deal and received tons of media coverage. They had a very talented guard named Marcus Evans. I rarely gave players their props, but Rice got a steal because this kid was a definitely high major talent. Coach never made me guard the best player. With the new foul rules, he didn't want me to get easy fouls nor did he want me to get fatigued since I carried the majority of the scoring load. We beat Rice by 4 points that year and I finished with 26 points. With every game we won, the bond between coach and I grew stronger.

Once the conference started, we had the best start in years. We won eight games straight and I was third in the league in scoring. We were tied for first place and we would finally play another one of the teams we were tied with, Stephen F. Austin Lumberjacks (SFA). They had the previous year's Player of the Year and Coach of the Year. They were a well-oiled machine, and it wouldn't be an easy match. Newspaper and media journalists interviewed us all that week. I was blessed to be the focal point of it. I had anywhere from seven to ten interviews, over the phone, in person, and on camera. All the questions were the same and everyone received similar answers. I talked about my team first, we knew how to set aside the egos and contribute where it was necessary to win. Then I gave the rest of the credit to our coach. Not only for providing me a scholarship and giving me a chance to continue to play basketball but for being a leader I could finally trust.

The game against SFA was magnified as tickets were sold out. All the news channels were there to cast the game and we were lucky enough to have home-court advantage. We prepared hard for them. They went to the NCAA tournament every year so it would be significant to beat them. The day of the game was like any other. We woke up, went to shoot around, watched the film, ate, and then rested before the game. On my walk to the stadium, I experienced something I never saw before at HBU. Two hours before the game started there were fans waiting to enter with a line wrapped around the outside. When I walked into the gym they had two sections filled with white and purple representing SFA and the other sections were for HBU fans. The entire gym was filled from tip-off. Our team played exceptionally well. Fans yelled and screamed as the game came down to the wire. At the last minute, we were down by two. We came down on offense and missed. When SFA got the ball someone from our bench said "foul." The rules that year where you could not foul a player without the ball. If it was done, it was deemed an intentional foul. They made both free throws and got the ball back. The lumberjacks won the game by six. The score was 72-66. I finished with 21 points, but it wasn't enough.

A couple of games later we lost our only center, who we ran the entire offense through. We struggled after that but still managed to finish fifth in the league. We played in the conference tournament and won the first game only to match back up with SFA. This time they beat us pretty badly. SFA went on to the Sweet 16 that year. We finished out the season by losing the first game in the CIT Post-Season Tournament, which ultimately is still a great accomplishment as a team. I finished that year averaging 17.6 points per game, 3.7 assists and 4.8 rebounds. I ranked third in the country for free throws attempts and third in the country for free throws made. I finished as the third-leading scorer in the Southland Conference averaging 20.1 points per game, 4.5 rebounds, and 3.9 assists. I was named First Team All-Southland, First Team all NABC, and HBU Male Athlete of the Year.

I wish my senior season had a different outcome. Just like high school, there were some players on my team who would never play another structured game. These were guys I cared about. Over time they became like my brothers. They grew on me and I built relationships with them that would last a lifetime. I attended four different schools and I had encounters with a lot of different players. I commend Coach Cottrell for recruiting respectful, religious, and highly educated individuals. He could have chosen better athletes, but he made sure each person signed to play fit his criteria. He put his dignity and pride over winning and I respected him for that. HBU wasn't the biggest school, they weren't in the best conference, and they didn't have the best facilities, but they gave me an opportunity, freedom to grow, and a chance to mature and further my basketball career. If someone would have told me while I was in high school, I would be at HBU five years later, I would have asked them to change their pharmacist. Houston Baptist University is the best thing that has ever happened to me, HBU is home. The dynamic of my college career is a true testament that you can't plan your destiny, it will never work how you intended, but that doesn't mean it can't be a happy ending,

After the season ended there was no time for breaks, I had a lot of things to figure out. First, I had to find out what agent I was going to have represent me. I was getting messages since my junior year and with the season I currently had a different agent was messaging me every day. I was told by multiple agents that acquiring a Nigerian passport would help me in the overseas recruitment process. The passport worked in Italy, Spain, and France. If you held a passport from an African country, you were considered a Cotonou player. In those three countries being a Cotonou would help because you wouldn't be considered an American. After the season, I decided to make a 12-hour trip to Atlanta, where the Consulate General of Nigeria is located.

The process of choosing an agent was difficult, they all said the same thing and I didn't have anyone to tell me what to look for. I was connected with a former NBA player named Gabe Muoneke. He praised his former agent and insisted that I sign with him. Although I didn't know Gabe for very long, he was a fellow Nigerian, and I knew I could trust him. The agent and I talked about my season and he told me to attend a Pro Day in Florida. He said he would use his connections to get me there and all I would have to do is show up. I had finally met an agent who could separate himself from everyone else with an opportunity.

I trained as hard as I ever had. I was already a hard worker, but I knew I had to work twice as hard as the guys who would be there since I was coming from a smaller school. I woke up daily and would go to the weight room for an hour, typically at 5 am. I was still using the university's facilities, so I wanted to make sure I didn't get in anyone's way. I would come back to the gym a couple of hours later and do a two-hour individual skill workout with my trainer Golden Corner. This part of my training usually took place anywhere from 10 am to 12 pm depending on gym availability, and would go for a two-hour duration. Then I would go home take a nap and come back to the gym at night to shoot for another two hours. I always made sure all the other teams at the school were finished with team workouts and I would isolate myself in the gym to shoot over and over and over again at 8 pm every night. I continued on that regimen for six weeks, Monday through Saturday, and rested only on Sundays.

CHAPTER 15
PRO DAY

On June 4th, I flew to Florida and drove to the IMG Academy. IMG is one of the best preparatory boarding schools in the country, with a world-renowned training facility. The Pro Day was scheduled for the following day. Some players had been training there since school ended. Top agencies would pay for players to work-out and train with certified instructors, these were usually guys who were going to the NBA. The agency would invest, hoping to get the money reimbursed after the player's first contract was signed.

When I landed, an Uber was there waiting to pick me up and transported me to the campus. The campus was massive, they had facilities for every sport. I checked in and immediately went to sleep. Early the next morning I received an email regarding my itinerary. In such short time, I had to learn things that guys had been getting trained on for months. The entire purpose of this day was to put everyone in the agency in front of NBA scouts. I was excited to meet the agent who made all of this possible. His name was Igor Crespo and he was a multi-millionaire based out of Spain. He had clients from all over but for the most part, he had high paid Latin clients who were either playing for high-level European clubs or playing in the NBA. His talk with me was very brief. He told me to 'play hard, work hard, and not be nervous.' I got a vibe that he wasn't as excited to meet me as I was to meet him, but with his clientele, I can see why.

We walked over to the weight room to prepare for our first series of tests. First, was our Anthropometric measurements. Various parts of our body were measured to evaluate how they compared with other NBA athletes. They measured the length and width of our hands, foot size, height with and without shoes, wings span, and weighed us. Next, we went to the weight room and did the bench press test. They put one hundred and eighty-five pounds and documented how many repetitions every individual could do. Shortly thereafter we performed a sequence of the performance test. All the tests were timed and documented and consisted of the vertical and max vertical jump, 10 and 20-yard dashes, lane agility, and lane shuffle. Before the event, I had not seen half of the drills, so the first time through I just did the best I could. I saw the guys who were most successful and studied their techniques. Quietly, I watched their footwork and hips, I saw what gave them an advantage and I mimicked it. The second time around I was applauded by the trainers for my quick improvements. Afterward they set aside two hours for us to eat and catch a quick nap. I went to eat and instead of napping, I opted for treatment. I thought rehab would be best for me since I was putting my body through strenuous routines it wasn't accustomed to.

The training room was connected to the gym and I could see the scouts walking in. After treatment, I walked into the gym to warm up. The gym was filled with at least one NBA scout from every team in the league. Three different groups were auditioning. My group was last and quite honestly it was the weakest of the three. The first group consisted of only two guys. After doing some research both players in that group had already played in the NBA. After them were two draft-eligible players who were projected first-round which included Juancho Hernangomez from Spain who was represented by Igor and the other was Skal Labissere from the University of Kentucky.

My group was last and instead of two, there were four of us. The reality was I had nothing to lose and everything to gain. I wasn't projected to get drafted, so there was no added pressure, but I still wanted to perform well. They split us up, guards and big men. On one end were the two big men and on the other end were the guards. We started with shooting, we shot 20 shots from five spots on the floor. There were three rebounders and a coach on each side. Coaches counted our makes and misses and documented it. After that, we went to shots of the move. They put us through different actions we would see in a game. At this point I had already exerted 60 percent of my energy. Last, was the live session where we would play three separate games to 6 points. Any other day this would have been easy but with the entire NBA watching I had to play in a gear that I wasn't aware I had. By the end of the three matches, I couldn't even see. I had to get pulled off the court, but I wasn't embarrassed, I had left everything out there.

That afternoon before flying back I decided to sign with Igor. He had the NBA clients and leverage and it would only make sense to sign with him. I hoped that with my talent and his connections he could land me a deal. The overseas recruitment didn't start until late June. The only people who would sign that early were guys signing back to the same team or NBA guys who were offered bigger contracts overseas. Most rookies didn't sign until late July/August after the veterans were chosen. I waited and worked out until I heard something. When I returned, I was introduced to a player who was actively playing overseas. He was the brother of one of my high school teammates. We worked out together and I gained a lot of knowledge on how the market worked. Chris Otule was another Houston native who went to Marquette University, he ended up playing for two years in Germany. He was home for the summer while he waited for his next contract. He mentioned the communication he and his agent had and how he would talk to him a couple of times a week. I never talked to Igor. I explained to Chris my situation and whom I signed with. He made it clear that I signed with a very reputable agent who had a lot of NBA clients and connections but he explained because of that I was probably low on his priority list. When I thought about it, Gabe made millions during his career, of course he and Igor were close. He made Igor lots of money, which led to their great relationship and I wasn't on that caliber.

An agent earns 10% commissions from an overseas contract, while if he is representing an NBA client, he earns 4%. After doing the math I gathered that if Igor was making 4 % of a thirty-million-dollar contract he wasn't going to be worried about 10% of a thirty thousand dollar contract. Most overseas contracts aren't great, especially for rookies. There is a massive false perception of the salary about overseas basketball. Players never really talked numbers. But everyone I knew acted like they made money or made references to getting a "bag." The longer I waited I grew furious and out of anger, I exploded on Igor in a message. Days went by without a response. I messaged him again, still no answer. I realized that if I couldn't get a hold of my agent when I had a question, I wouldn't be able to get a hold of him when something went wrong in a foreign country. I knew I had made a bad decision. More days went by with still no response. Finally, he called me back and expressed his frustration because I called him so much. He explained to me that the market for rookies is small. Like a business, if someone owned a company, as an employer/business owner, they would want older and more experienced employees. It was the same with basketball. Basketball clubs didn't want young guys, they wanted experienced players who knew how the European game was played. He told me he had a team for me and then explained there wouldn't be much money involved. Since Igor was used to dealing with million-dollar clients, when he referred to "not much money" I thought it was still going to be a decent amount. The team in Spain was a second league offering $1,200 a month for a nine-month season. I couldn't believe what I was hearing. Immediately out of anger I told him, I averaged 20 points that year and if the best he could do was get me $1,200, I wanted to sign a termination agreement. I immediately signed with another reputable agency that was previously interested in me.

July turned to August and I heard nothing. At least with these guys, they contacted me at the end of every week to let me know their progress. Chris Otule and I both stressed the entire month. He hadn't got a job either and he played in Top League Germany, so I knew it wasn't just happening to me. The hardest part about the industry is to train day in and day out not knowing when or if that contract would ever come. But every day I got up and went to the gym. One morning I lost my partner in crime, Chris called and told me he would be going to a team in France. I was genuinely happy for him, we had built a unique rapport after such a short time. He would leave the following week and I would stay in Houston. *How did this happen to me? I thought I had a great season*, I worried. I would have sleepless nights asking myself a million questions. I would search EuroBasket all day and night. EuroBasket is the main online source that informed guys "who and where" a player was signed to. It was the first thing that popped up when I opened my internet browser because I searched it so much. It seemed like every day there was a new player signing. The end of August came and I had to move out of my HBU apartment. I packed up my things and moved back into my mom's house. I didn't unpack though; I was optimistic any day would be my day. Late August turned into September, then September turned into October. At this time, I was contemplating giving up. I got into multiple arguments with my agents and I was beyond frustrated because it seemed as if everyone was signing but me.

Essentially this is how it all worked:

European teams consisted of 12 players per roster. In most leagues, there are 12-15 teams per league. Most countries consist of only one league. The bigger countries sometimes have 2 or 3 leagues. Of those teams, most leagues have 2-3 imports. Imports are American players. The rest of the team would be primarily made up of domestic players from a country. Of those 2-3 Americans on the team, one of the positions would be a guard and guys were lucky if the team wanted a first-year player (rookie). Only the low budgeted teams wanted young guys since they didn't have the money to pay more experienced players. Player's first contract would be the lowest due to a lack of experience. European teams will use whatever they can to reduce the amount of money they have to pay a player.

There is a certain window for rookie recruitment and I missed that window because Igor wasn't doing his job. He specifically only sent my profile to Spanish teams. Spain is one of the best countries for basketball, but he was limiting me by only sending my profile to one country. When I switched agents in August a lot of teams had already signed their guys and were ready to bring them in for pre-season. From late August to early October teams would make cuts of the players who didn't fit the criteria they initially wanted. In pre-season, some players would pack their belongings for eight to nine months. Not playing well or getting hurt would result in being terminated and returned to the states. When they would make a cut the last thing a team would want to do is bring in a guy who had no experience in the middle of October. I had no offers, no inquires, and no money.

My depression grew, I would have more sleepless nights. I seldom answered my phone and some days I didn't eat. I hit the pinnacle of depression and I didn't know what to do. Consequently, I switched agents again in the belief that something would change. Agents would message me asking me why I wasn't signed. Then they would say they could get me a deal, when I switched, they had me doing the same thing I was doing before, waiting. I had gone through three agents without playing one game overseas. I resorted back to my old college mentality of transferring when I hit adversity. I was doing the same thing with the overseas process.

Athlete	Anthropometric Measurements							Performance Tests							
	Hand Span	Hand Length	Wing Span	Height w/s	Height w/os	Reach	Weight	Vertical Jump	Max Vertical	10 yd, 20 yd, 3/4 Court			Lane Shuttle	Lane Agility	185 Bench
Elgin Cook	10.5	8 3/4	6'11 1/8"	78 1/4	77	97	215	133	140	1.77	2.86	3.3	2.53	11.32	18
Shaq Goodwin	9 3/8	9	71"	80.5	79.25	102.5	243.2	133.5	139	1.98	3.15	3.7	2.72	12.08	8
Kyle Collinsworth	9 1/8	8	66 7/8"	78.75	77.75	99	216	129.5	135.5	1.69	2.83	3.4	2.53	10.95	8
Jaleel Cousins	9 3/8	9 1/2	76 3/8"	82.25	81.37	109	256.8	135.5	139.5	1.81	3.08	3.68	2.92	12.35	12
Ilja Gromovs	10 3/4	9 1/8	73 3/8"	83.5	82.5	107	235.6	135.5	139	1.8	3.08	3.57	2.76	12.63	12
Jamari Traylor	8 3/4	8 3/4	69 1/4"	80.5	79.5	101.5	219.6	133	138	1.76	2.87	3.45	2.81	11.78	16
Torrance Rowe	7 3/4	7 1/2	61 1/4"	72.5	71.12	90	151.6	118.5	126	1.65	2.8	3.32	2.43	10.98	1
Anthony Odunsi	8 5/8	8 1/4	66 3/8"	76	75	96	204.8	126.5	132.5	1.6	2.75	3.27	2.47	11.49	12
Boubacar Moungoro	9 1/8	9 1/4	7	78.25	77.25	101	203	132	137.5	1.64	2.8	3.31	2.87	11.74	12
Devin Cherry	8 3/4	8 1/2	66 3/8"	74.87	74	95.25	196	126	129.5	1.73	2.89	3.46	2.66	11.52	14

IMG ACADEMY — NBA
Relativity Pro Day Testing Results

Statistics from 2016 NBA Pro Day at IMG Academy

CHAPTER 16
NBA G LEAGUE

My new agent explained to me that I had great stats, but I was still a rookie and the fact that I missed the recruiting process due to Igor wasn't good, but that we couldn't dwell on it. He sent me an alternate route and I entered my name into the 2016 NBA G League draft. He explained that it was to my benefit to attend the tryouts that were nearby. I lived in Houston. The Houston Rockets, San Antonio Spurs, and Dallas Mavericks all had G League teams in the vicinity. He did warn me that the camps were also open to the public so anyone who had $150 could tryout. If you were a reputable player and draft-eligible, then your entry fee was waived. The first camp was the Rockets G League team also known as the Rio Grande Valley Vipers. Followed by the Austin Spurs which was the San Antonio Spurs G League team. Then Texas legends, which was the last of the camps, but it would be the following week.

The opening day of the Viper's camp arrived. My agent told me I would be waived financially for all camps, all I had to do was perform. When I arrived, the gym was full of people. We stretched, shot, and then immediately played games. There were about 250 players in attendance, they separated thirty of the best which I was a part of. Of the thirty, the coaches split us up into three teams where we would specifically play each other, that way the scouts could see who they wanted. This was their way of separating the actual talent from the fundraiser they were partially running. I was 6'4", with very average athleticism compared to some of the players. There was not much I could do to stick out, half the time guys were so selfish I would go possessions without touching the ball. Players that were usually successful in these settings were big guys, those that were abnormally large and could do things others physically couldn't. 6'4" might seem tall to the average person but in the basketball world, it's a common height, if anything it's on the shorter side. The camp finished at around 9 pm and from there I drove straight to Austin. I stayed at a friend's house and with less than six hours of sleep, I went to the next camp. It was the same set-up but this time I didn't get to be a part of the talented players who were separated from the rest. It was an entire day wasted and I had to drive three and a half hours back to Houston after a whole day of camp. The drives back were the worst as I rehashed the events that took place; hitting myself in the head in frustration on how I could have shot a shot or attacked there. I was my own hardest critic.

The Legends Camp was by invitation only. There were 25 players in total. I performed well there and thought I might get an opportunity to get picked up with them. I didn't want to go to the G League, it was too political. They only wanted big named players and guys who had been affiliated with the program prior. Nonetheless, the month of October gave me hope. It was a reason to get up and continue working out. The draft was set for Sunday, October 30th. I went to church and acted as if it was a normal day while I tried not to stress myself out. When I walked out, I had texts from everyone congratulating me on getting drafted. I was taken 5th round 93rd overall to the Canton Charge of the 2016 NBA G League draft. My agent told me to expect some calls from the General Manager (GM) and that I shouldn't get my hopes high because they usually cut 80 percent of the guys they draft. Only one or two made the team from the players they drafted. The GM and president both called from the Canton Charge and told me what to expect. I was told to pack a bag, and that I would be leaving the next morning. I asked my agent if I should pack as if was going to stay there for the entire season. He told me to pack for a couple of weeks and if I made the team, to ship my remaining clothes. I was new to the process, but I could tell the chances of making it were slim. His job wasn't to be overly optimistic. He was my agent, I needed him to be honest.

The training camp lasted for about three weeks. Some teams were more ruthless than others. Some teams cut guys the first day and some teams kept players the entire camp. The Canton Charge were led by former Duke Blue Devil, Quin Cook. Cook and I played the same position. I was a lot bigger, so it was in my best interest to be versatile because I knew I wasn't going to take his spot. He was the franchise player. After a couple of days, I knew I wouldn't make the team. It became obvious in the scrimmages because I would be one of the last players to get in the game. I messaged my agent about what was going on and he responded, 'Just keep getting paid.' It was a business, every day I showed up to practice it was money in my pocket. When I figured I was going to get cut, that became the most important thing, money. It was a couple of days before the tip-off of the season and I was still in Canton, Ohio. We had an open scrimmage and right after I was called into the office. I stood there in front of the GM who looked like he fired people for a living. He stared directly into my eyes, with no remorse, and said, 'Thanks for coming, your assistance would no longer be needed.' He went further to tell me my return flight was set for the next morning at 6 am. I was welcomed to my first experience of getting cut from basketball and my next "wake up call." It was single-handedly the most ruthless, nonchalant situation I had ever witnessed. I knew at that very moment; basketball would never be the same. I flew back home to Houston and sat upright on the couch all night. When I failed, I would punish my mind and body, I was so upset. I didn't know how to handle adversity.

My family dynamics had changed. My mom remarried and moved to Nigeria so it was only my sister and me at home. My mom found out about my return home and asked me to work at her office. She said she needed someone at the front desk. I agreed without hesitation and for the next two months, I reported for work on Monday-Friday from 9 am-5 pm. It was an outlet for me to make a little money and to get my mind off things. After work, I would go straight to the gym. I became accustomed to the long schedule. Some days were harder than others but even on my worst days I still trained after sitting in an office for hours. I was in a dark place and was barely surviving mentally. There were a couple of people who would constantly check in on me. Chris was one of them, he would call every day. I always expressed my stress of the industry and asked questions about why he thought I was still at home. I imagine he got tired of it, but every day he made sure he called and that's when our friendship elevated. True friendship does not get discovered when things are going well, and everyone is happy. It gets discovered when one of the individuals hit rock bottom and the other is there to lift them.

One morning while at work I received a call from my agent. He told me there was a team in Greece interested in me. I had heard some stories about how unreliable Greece could be with monthly wages but that wasn't at the top of my mind. My excitement level grew, and I instantly called my mom with the news. The agent asked if I would take two thousand per month and at that time I was desperate anything would suffice. He asked me to send him a copy of my passport. I was working, so I had my sister forward it over. That was the last thing I heard from my agent that day. There was no follow-up text and no confirmation, so I assumed they were still in the process of negotiating. The following morning, I still didn't hear anything. After growing impatient, I messaged my agent asking him for an update on the situation. He said unfortunately they had found someone else because he hadn't heard from them after sending the documentation. Teams receive hundreds of profiles from agents of different players every day. A profile consists of a player's resume and film. I guess the team ran across a player they felt would be a better fit. The overseas world is ruthless, they don't care about morals or ethics. I was told that a lot of teams made changes around December. If they were unhappy with a player's production, they would make a change, so I waited.

Anthony Odunsi gets drafted to the Canton Charge in the 2016 G League draft.

(Cleveland Cavaliers affiliate team)

CHAPTER 17
ICELAND

It was December, Christmas was nearing and weeks went by without any news. I was still having sleepless nights, while checking my phone and email all day and night. I even picked up another bad habit and started to look at my highlight tape to see if the views were going up so I would know if someone was watching it or not. I was losing it mentally, but I kept enough composure so people couldn't tell. One morning I received a message from an agent that didn't represent me. He was an NBA agent and didn't hold a FIBA (Overseas) license. He asked if I was still unemployed and mentioned he had a team that may be interested in me. He said an Icelandic coach asked him for a player and I fit the exact criteria. I gave him permission to send my profile and we waited. I knew this agent wasn't just showing acts of kindness, there was an agent fee in it for him. In this business no one on that level did things because it was the right thing, the motive was always financial gain. If it wasn't me, he would have messaged some other player, from some other state trying to get him signed. That's what agents did. If they had a relationship with a coach, they would go out and find players who weren't a part of their agency and try to sign them to a team. Once a player was signed, the agent fee was collected and most times the player would never hear from the agent again. Sometimes these agents wouldn't even want the player to sign with them and be a part of their agency, they just wanted the money.

At this point I knew not to get my hopes up, I would just be hurting myself in the long run. I moved back into the dorms at HBU. Instead of driving every day to the gym to work out, I stayed on campus. One of my teammates from the previous year had an extra room he used for storage, he lived off-campus with his girlfriend and gave me a place to live. There was a bed in there and it was more convenient, so I put it to use. The room was filled with their stuff. Clothes, shoes and golf clubs were everywhere, it wasn't ideal, but it worked since I only needed a bed. I also ate at the cafeteria; I was frugal, and it was my way of being cost-efficient. I would try and be discrete, but people would always spot me out and ask me why I was on campus. I knew no one would understand the situation or how everything worked so I spent most days trying to be unseen and avoiding texts. I was embarrassed by my journey. I did so well at HBU, people thought I was going to do big things and it was hard to face my reality.

I received a friend request from a random guy on Facebook after one of my workouts. He was from Iceland and we had a ton of friends in common, all of whom were athletes. I figured he was probably the coach. He added me but never said anything. A couple of days later he messaged me and told me he liked my game and that he needed to make a change on his team. He signed a big man but after months of playing, he realized that he had made the wrong decision. I researched the details of the team and found the player. He was a 34-year-old power forward. He wasn't having a bad season nor was the team losing. At the time they were in second place in the league. I'm a firm believer if it's not broken don't fix it but this could have potentially been my first deal. I wasn't worried about their internal issues. Over the next couple of days, he would message me questions about my personal life. He was a bit eerie and was probably bored. He also asked to reach out to my college coach, so I was glad I had a great relationship with him. Coaches, general managers, and presidents would reach out to old coaches, it was in a player's best interest to have a solid relationship with them. I never mentioned anything to my agent, he couldn't find me a deal, so this wasn't any of his business. When they finally offered, I messaged my agent and told him. He disrespectfully talked about how it wasn't the best league and I would be a fool to take the offer. He explained Europe is very political and that general managers and teams were very judgmental on certain leagues. I knew Iceland wasn't the best league but it was better than the "stay at home league" – that was the worst league on Earth. The offer was for $2,100 a month and more money than most rookies were getting. They offered me accommodations, Wi-Fi, a car, and a couple of meals a week at a local restaurant. I was a numbers guy but only when it came to my own personal money. Food in some of the countries was so expensive for a player to get a couple of free meals a week was equivalent to adding a couple of hundred dollars to the contract. I ran it by some people, and they talked about how good the offer was, but that the league wasn't well respected. I could either take the for sure or wait for the unknown. I signed my first contract and I set to leave America the day after Christmas. My family was excited for me, but they told me they were worried I wasn't mentally stable. I asked my mom if she knew who was going to replace me at her job and she told me she didn't need me there. The only reason she offered me the job was because she didn't want me at home all day with an idle mind. That was typical for my mom, she always put my sister and I first. She was my hero.

I arrived on December 28th in Reykjavik, Iceland. I was the only black person on the flight, there was nothing but blonde-haired, white people. We walked from the plane to the train that took us to the actual airport. While in transit, I experienced some of the worst weather conditions I had experienced in my life. It was freezing and the winds were enough to move a parked car. I don't recall what time it was, I just remember it being pitch-black. Iceland just like the other Scandinavian countries had minimal amounts of sunlight. During December, it was a maximum of five hours per day, and depending on your sleeping regime you may have missed it. As I walked into the airport, I saw that everything was written in Icelandic. It was an English-speaking country, but the airport was a complete throw off. As I approached the baggage claim, I came to find out that my bags were left behind on my connecting flight. I had been flying for almost 18 hours, now I would have to remain in the same clothes for another day. When I walked out from the baggage claim, the coach arrived to pick me up. His name was Hrafn Kristjánsson. I couldn't pronounce his name, therefor referred to him as coach. He recognized me from my pictures but I'm sure it wasn't hard for him to pick me out from the crowd. We drove about an hour back to Gardobaer, it was a wealthy suburb in Reykjavik. He pulled up to a big two-story house that looked like an old cabin. There was someone else living there but he was off on holiday. Coach told me to get some rest and that we would have practice later that night. I expressed to him that I didn't have any of my clothes and he said that he would get some guys on the team to figure it out. Many of the guys on the team worked regular jobs, so practice was at night.

Most beginner-level countries were like that. The Americans who would come over were the full-time pros and the domestic player was the semi-pros. There were exceptions. If there was a domestic player who was just as good as an American, they would pay him well. Those guys were very essential to teams and there weren't many. We had one on my team who was allegedly earning almost triple what I was.

I showed up at the gym around 8:30 pm for a 9 pm practice. The locker room was small and old with showers and a little fisher-price looking pool used as an ice tub. I quickly figured out European amenities weren't as updated as what I was used to. There were some tights and old crumbled socks waiting for me. Luckily, I had packed my shoes in my backpack or they might have given me sandals to wear out there. I didn't take the tights. I wasn't wearing another man's undergarment. I took the socks and headed out to the gym. The gym was in a tiny arena with six baskets. They had the main two goals across from each other with glass backboards, and the other four were on the sides with wooden backboards. This was one of the best clubs in Iceland, I thought they would have more to offer. After all that I had been through to get to this point, I was just grateful for the opportunity. I was introduced to the team. Coach Kristjánsson would talk to them in Icelandic and talk to me in English. This particular league only had one American. Some teams would have two, it would be a situation where one import would play half the game and the other player would play the other half. I grieved for players in this situation, it was a difficult system to be successful in.

The practice was always simple but long and hard. We would warm up with some type of team drill. 3 on 2, 2 on 1, or 3-man weave. We played live games for hours and then would shoot. They had a simple offense, so I picked up on it quickly. By the time practice would end it was almost midnight. We practiced every day and lifted weights once a week. The lifting was intense, the strength and conditioning coach was an ex-handball player.

I waited for about a week until I was able to get all my items squared away. Everyone on staff worked on a volunteer basis, it was like a hobby for them. Consequently, it took some time for them to get me all setup. The GM took me to pick up the car I would be using over the next couple of months. When we arrived at the rental place, it was at the front waiting. It was a small bright yellow hatchback, which was a common European car. Most teams gave Americans a stick shift, I didn't know how to drive one, so I got lucky they gave me an automatic. After the car purchase, we went to the mall to set up a bank account. The arrangement was to pay me monthly in their foreign currency, Icelandic Krona, and at the end of the season, I could transfer the money back to USD. The American dollar was almost double the Krona. The pay seemed pretty decent until I used the conversion rate to figure out what I was getting paid.

The general manager took me on a little tour of the town and then dropped me off, because I didn't know my way around they had an employee drop my new car off at my house. The days blended in together. The overseas life is repetitive to the point where I would never know what day it was. The practice wasn't until 9 pm and I would have the entire day to myself. Most days I would sit at home, sleep, and watch Netflix because everything was so costly I didn't go out much. I received the occasional calls from friends and family checking in on me. To switch up my routine, I would try and go to the gym to shoot but there was always something going on there. It was hard at first adjusting to everything, but eventually, I got used to it. One thing I never got used to was the weather. Iceland had extreme weather conditions during the winter. I was too scared to drive the first month so I would beg my teammates to pick me up. There was snow higher than I had ever seen, and it piled up around my car. When I finally drove my car for the first time, myself and two others spent hours digging it out of the snow. I only drove to essential places like the grocery store, the gym, or the weight room. If it wasn't one of those places, I didn't feel there was a reason to leave.

Our first game was around the corner. I didn't know the names of the other teams, where they ranked, or anything else. I just tried to focus on my job and that was to win and put-up numbers. There was a lot of pressure on the Americans to handle the scoring load. I was nervous days before the first game. I knew I had just replaced a 34-year-old man, clearly the coach didn't have any remorse. I thought if I didn't play well, he would send me home as well. Game days were the complete opposite of college. They just told us to show up about an hour before game time. What a player ate or did before the game was up to him. There was no shootaround and we watched a film at the beginning of the week. Half of the time I didn't understand what they were talking about anyway.

Hours before tip-off, my coach came to my house and told me my papers didn't go through. I was on a working visa and if it wasn't cleared quick enough, I wasn't allowed to play. He was positive that I would be cleared the following week. I dressed up in a polo and went to cheer my team. It worked out to my benefit; I had a chance to dissect the game in person. The biggest differences between overseas basketball and American basketball is the speed and the style of play.

In Europe they were more strategic, their players were less athletic. They played off IQ and structure. In America, we played more of an individual type of basketball. Purely off athleticism and speed. Iceland was like the battle of the "fathers," there were a bunch of old and strong men in the league. It didn't play toward our advantage as Americans. I felt the league was prejudice toward us. We never received any calls after getting beat up the entire game. I struggled, that was my style of play, my entire life I was known to create contact and shoot free throws. I had to adjust. We went on to win that game. I was hoping guys on the team would introduce me to the nightlife, but they were all older. There were four players around my age and two were in serious relationships. The other two were single, but that particular night they went home.

We played once a week and it was always on a Saturday evening. Every week consisted of the same thing, practice Monday-Friday from 9-11 pm with Mondays lifting weights. The amount of free time was mind-boggling, but I adjusted. The next game rolled around, and it was an away match. Iceland was small so we didn't travel far. We arrived at the facility about an hour and a half before the game. My entire college career I taped my ankles before games, but when I asked my teammate for the trainer, he said, "He only comes to home games." Some of the other players learned to tape themselves. Europeans also didn't use pre-wrap so when I did get taped it was miserable trying to get it off.

Our coach was passionate, he got us wired up with his pre-game speeches. We broke the huddle out and prepared for the tip-off. The game started and anxiety was high. This was my first overseas game, in a country where I had no relatives, friends, or family members in close proximity. After a couple of trips down the court, I gained my second wind. I touched the ball every time down the floor, I also never came out. In college, my coach liked to play guys evenly, so I took full advantage of all the playing time. There was no scouting report out on me, no one knew what to expect. The game went down to the last second and the coach put the ball in my hands and told me to go 1 on 1. I ended up turning the ball over late in the shot clock and we lost. They had only lost one game up until that point and in my first game we lost. I finished with 22 points, 9 rebounds, and 4 assists. I went home and didn't sleep well that night, scared that they would send me home. My coach wasn't worried about my statistics, he cared about wins. We then lost our next game, which my coach blamed on me. I almost felt he had unrealistic expectations. It's like he thought Americans weren't human.

After the second games film, we had a meeting. He asked me to stay. He sat me down and asked me how I thought I was playing. I told him I only played two games, but that I'm still trying to get a feel for everything. He looked at me and said, 'You are leading the team in points, and second in rebounds but we are losing and if we don't start winning, I don't know what I'm going to do.' The pressure to perform in sports is uncanny. Often it is what causes players to quit. I experienced it from when I was young until my college days, however, the pressure of playing professionally is indescribable. Especially since there was only one import in Iceland. If there were more Americans, the attention would be diversified.

The next game came around and we played one of the better teams in the league. I started off the game hot but right before halftime we had one of our best players go down with a concussion. He had a history with them, so they sent him home right away. When we started the second half, I sensed a little more added pressure and I rose to the occasion. We ended up winning the game by four. It was a heated match and we were able to make some key shots. I finished with 27 points, 9 rebounds, and 6 assists. My coach grabbed and hugged me. We all celebrated in the locker room. I knew I had bought myself some more time. I lived for the games we won, and I played well in. That game was huge, so I thought guys would go out, but they didn't. I asked the two younger guys if they wanted to go out, but they said 'No.' I went home and watched movies. I found out the following Monday that the guys who told me they didn't want to go out, actually did go out and just didn't tell me. It was hard being an outcast just because I was the only American.

As time went on my knowledge of the overseas industry grew and I found out it was very political and strategic. Iceland wasn't the most respected league, but it also wasn't the worst either. The only guys who got moved up were the ones who dominated statistical categories or the ones that won championships. There was no in-between, it was one or the other. I would spend all night researching guys who played in the league in the previous years and where they went after. That would give me a good idea of what countries were looking and which weren't. The guys who didn't play well got stuck and had no upward mobility.

The first season was the most important. If a player played well, another team would sign him but if he didn't there was a high possibility he would stay at the same level of struggle to get another contract. The more I researched, the more stressed I became which consequently led me to have bad games, it was psychological for me and I was putting too much pressure on myself. My coach noticed and gave me less playing time and stopped communicating with me. I started to feel resentment, not because I had an attitude or because I was a bad teammate. I just wasn't satisfying what he felt the team needed.

I was making a huge sacrifice, thousands of miles from home and everyone I knew and loved, and it was taking a toll on me physically, mentally, and emotionally. I was shut into my house for twenty hours out of the day. I either walked around the malls or would go to the grocery store as a coping mechanism. Going out triggered abnormal stares from Icelanders. They were very respectful but they were infatuated with people who looked different. Some of them lived their entire life, and never encountered a person from another race. After months I started to look unkept. Although back home I usually cut my hair, due to the voltage difference and the lack of cultural diversity I didn't have the devices to cut my hair. Instead, I lined my edges up with a razor blade. I also used the same method in my pubic area but broke out ferociously due to skin irritation. *I decided to never do that again.* I was low maintenance; I understood the opportunity that was given to me and tried to make the most of the situation but when the basketball environment became hostile, it made my day to day living difficult.

I believe at times my coach wanted me to quit. Some of the management and coaching staff of the European teams didn't want Americans there, they just knew they need them to win. I felt my teammates resented me as a result of my coach's behavior. My childhood life prepared me for this. Growing up in wealthy neighborhood I feel like people expected me to act a certain way because of my skin color. I understood that early and I never fed into the stereotypes. I never wanted to validate people's ignorance, so I always made sure I did the right thing, I made sure I handled myself first class and if anyone was going to say anything bad about me it wouldn't be about my character. That was something I could control.

I had my biggest game of the year against the league's first-place team. They had a big budget and were able to put together the best roster in the league without a doubt. They were in the first place and we were in second. We had no way of winning the league. It was the final game of the conference play before finals and they were two games up on us. From the jump ball, I showed my value. My coach was cheering me on, pumping his fist and telling me, 'You got it.' When things were going well, he was my best friend. When they were going bad, I'm sure he had the airline on speed dial threatening to send me back. The game was pretty even throughout. It seemed like every couple of minutes one of our teams took the lead. By the fourth quarter, I was a couple of points away from a twenty point game. In Europe, twenty point games weren't easy to come by. I came down one possession and hit a three right in front of the opposing team's bench. As the leather from the ball went through the net, I yelled at their bench and coach. Some may call it enthusiastic or passionate behavior, but the yelling didn't have anything to do with the game. The yell was an exchange for my daily frustration in a foreign environment. My yell was fueled with anger and sadness for being all alone in a place where I felt people wanted me to fail. They only saw the surface and as I jogged back, my team waved towels and screamed. During those forty minutes, they always had my back, after the games I wasn't so sure. We won the game that night. The first time they played, before my arrival they lost. I won't say I was the difference, but I will say I am glad it is documented.

I stopped asking my teammates to go out and that night I went out by myself. A night out was expensive from all angles. Alcoholic beverages were ridiculously priced because they were imported. A normal bottle I would purchase back home would range from $20 to $55. In Iceland, $60 was the minimum you would pay for bottom-shelf liquor. It was outrageous, to save some money I would find someone traveling in the country and ask them to buy and bring the liquor with them. I would later compensate them for the purchase and their labor once they arrived in the country. The cab fee was even more inflated, a trip to the bars and back would be around $70. It was expensive but sitting in the house grew old. I'm sure some players would spend their entire month's wages on partying. There was a street of bars in downtown Reykjavik where I would always see the imports hanging out. Some were together and some were alone. I usually did my own thing although I preferred being around a group to help make things less awkward. But sometimes being a minority in Iceland had its benefits. I would always make friends when I went out and I felt like a celebrity at times. You would think people were intrigued because I played basketball. That wasn't it. It was actually because I was African-American and when it came to women in their early twenties, I assumed they wanted to engage in a fantasy. The main nightclub was called B5. They were the club that played urban music and wouldn't close until 6 am. I enjoyed the nightlife there. It was refreshing. In America, specifically, Houston where I am from, people try to fit an image or be perceived a certain way. In Iceland people just had fun. If a woman wanted to buy you a drink she would, the narrative was different.

The playoffs were next, we were matched up against IR Reykjavik (IR). We were a higher seed, so we got home-court advantage. We played them my first game in League Play and lost. The series was best out of five. The matches would be played every two days. The preparation was a bit different. I knew there was more money on the table. In my contract, I had incentives that stated for every round won, I would receive a bonus, and every round the incentive would increase. Icelanders took these games seriously. It was night and day from League Play to playoffs. The first game against IR I could barely see, there was smoke everywhere with fans yelling and chanting. The atmosphere was indescribable. The player who was hurt earlier in the season came back and helped us in many ways. We beat them three times straight. I saw my playing time significantly decrease and if I messed up, the coach would immediately take me out. I persevered through and still averaged 17 points throughout the first round of matches. The second series was against Grindavik. This team was flat out more talented than us and it showed. They swept us. After they won two games straight my coach decided it was my fault we were losing and took me out of the starting lineup. I was the "professional" so they were not going to blame it on the player getting paid pennies. I kept my composure when I received the bad news. Once the next game started, I was one of the last guys to sub in. The coach was trying to make a statement and it didn't work- we lost the final game by thirty. We walked into the locker room and everyone sat quietly. One by one everyone hugged and departed. Once I left that stadium, I never spoke to my coach again.

Overseas can get complicated and I finally understood why so much internal investigation was done before my arrival. European teams have a budget, which includes player wages, personal travel, accommodation, food, and team travel. The coaches and general managers of the teams would recruit a player and negotiate a salary for the entire year. Recruiting was done by either statistical data or from watching a highlight reel/ full game film. They would budget two plane tickets for the year for the import to the country and back home. Each plane ticket overseas was no less than one thousand dollars. In most situations, tickets were booked last minute so it could have probably cost more. Depending on the season, teams would try to bring in a better player later and this would cost additional money. Since the teams were cheap, early on they would try and get a cheap inexperienced player. If they were on the fringe of being in or out of the playoffs, they would cut the cheap player and bring in a more experienced player. The motive behind a coach and player is obvious. The coach's job is to win. More money for him and his family, while being subject to an extension on his contract.

For the player, the moment he takes off on the plane his mind is fixated on production, playing well enough to move up in leagues. A player is always worried about the next step, the next league. As a player, I could never enjoy where I was. I was always concerned about the following year before I got there. From the moment I got into Iceland, I was worried about what was next because I thought I deserved better. People would tell me it wasn't a good enough league, so I worried about leaving more than I did enjoying my time there. I looked up and it was all over. I left Iceland a couple of days after our last game. I averaged 16.6 points per game, 6 rebounds and 3 assists on the second-place team in the league. I received all my money and returned everything the way it was given to me. I thanked the GM for giving me my first opportunity. I left Iceland and flew to France to visit Chris for a short vacation before going back home.

I arrived at the airport gate and boarded the plane but while walking to my seat I noticed that my pockets were light. I couldn't find my wallet. Immediately, I started shuffling through my bag. Everyone on the plane was staring at me in confusion. I expressed to the flight attendant that I misplaced my wallet and I thought it might be on the floor at the gate. They restricted me from going to look myself, I knew I would have searched more thoroughly than he did. The flight attendant left to look, only to come back two minutes later with bad news. I didn't sleep the entire plane ride. My firsts stop was London. After I turned on my phone, I received messages from my mom saying some lady contacted her about my wallet. She found my license and looked my name up on Facebook. She then messaged everyone with the same last name. She also messaged me saying who she was, where she was from, and that she had my wallet. She explained she found it at the gate but didn't want to turn it into the desk because she felt they would have taken the money inside. It was the kindest act by a person I had ever experienced. Talking to her calmed my nerves. She said she would send the wallet to France so I could enjoy my vacation. I sent her the address and she kept her word.

When I arrived in Cannes, France, Chris picked me up from the airport and we drove to Antibes. The South of France was beautiful. It reminded me of Miami with all the palm trees and beautiful beaches. It was a game day for him, so we went straight back to his apartment. He lived in a two-bedroom apartment by himself. After a nap, he prepared for his game. Upon arrival to the arena, we pulled up to a gate with a guard in front asking for identification. As we pulled in, I saw other team cars with the team logo. There were five, one for each American import. We were almost two hours early. I didn't have any other way of getting there, so I had to arrive when the other players did but I didn't mind, I liked to be around basketball.

The stadium was huge, it could probably sit a couple of thousand people. Fashion was prominent in France, the players dressed up in blazers and nice shirts before the game. I wore sweats and a winter jacket to all my games in Iceland to make sure I didn't freeze in route to the gym. One by one the players started going inside the locker room to change. After they started warming up I quickly noticed the difference in size and athletic ability compared to my league. It was the difference between a beginner league and one of the better leagues in Europe. To put it in perspective a French player on his team was drafted by the Atlanta Hawks and because he wasn't quite ready yet, they let him come back to France and play another year. The league was called Pro-A and it was well respected. The introduction was impressive with flashing lights, horns blaring, mascots, and cameras flashing. It was night and day from the Icelandic league. The style of the game was the same throughout Europe, very slow and strategic. Teams came down and ran the offense every time down to the end of the shot clock.

The average European player is less athletic than an American player, that's why they play off of IQ and we play off of athletic ability. Chris's team wasn't very good, but he was having a breakout season. They ended up winning that game which set the mood for a night out. After the game, the players signed autographs and talked to the fans. We arrived at Chris's apartment and immediately changed clothes. All his teammates came over and we got ready to go out for the night. The team structure was different in France, teams were allowed four Americans and a Cotonou. He and the other Americans were close, communicating at all times by a group chat. It was easier when you had other Americans on your team, everything didn't feel as foreign which equated to less lonely nights. The nightlife was great, at least what I could remember of it.

The next day we drove to Cannes, another suburb in the south of France. The landscape was breathtaking, it was life on an island. The beach was beautiful, with blue water. We hung out and relaxed for hours. Afterward, I flew back to America to figure out my next move. Chris had about a month left before his season was over. He had signed a contract in China for their summer league before his season was even up. Chris was 6'11" and graduated from Marquette University, the combination of height and politics from a BCS school played to his favor. It was a game of supply and demand. There were only a few 7" players who were mobile and healthy. There was a high demand for players his size.

I flew back to Houston and started the process all over again. I would train all summer while waiting for my agent to find me another job. People thought finding a rookie a job was hard, it's even harder to find a player a second job if the player didn't have a breakout season. I was hopeful that summer would be different than the previous. I hoped that because I had European stats on my resume people would take a chance on me, but it was the complete opposite, it actually made it more difficult for my recruiting.

CHAPTER 18
NIGERIAN NATIONAL TEAM

I returned in April and took the rest of the month off. Early June I started working out again. I would rehab, watch films, and have a rigorous skill work session. During this time, I wasn't getting paid. I wanted to take my game to the next level so I hired a trainer. The narrative on the overseas world was that players got paid for nine months, the three months remaining at home, they would live off what they made that season. If you were paid a low salary, which most were, it wasn't much to live off of.

This time around my agent was transparent. He said it was going to be hard to find me another job that I wanted, due to my performance in Iceland. He said I was lucky to get paid the amount I did.

The overseas market is full of players of all ages, sizes, and positions. Every year there are more players than the last, due to guys coming in from college. The lower-level jobs were the hardest because they had the highest number of candidates up for it. If it was between me and a college player and the team liked us equally they would oftentimes go with the college player because they knew he would be cheaper and take less money. There were even scenarios where a player would get a job over another player because he offered to pay for the plane ticket. Recruitment was exhausting. No one wanted to be taken advantage of. It was better to take less, than not take anything at all. The higher-level of a player you were the less advantage they could take because there were only so many players that fit the resume criteria. I compared it to a company and an entry-level job. Essentially an entry-level job can bring almost anyone in and teach them how things work. But as an employee works his way up to higher-level jobs like a manager or supervisor, the company would have to compensate them accordingly to make sure the job was done correctly. Therefore, not everyone could qualify for higher-level jobs. I was still at the beginner level jobs and the market was full of players like me.

Instead of returning home and using the money I had saved, I picked up a job I enjoyed at Triumph Sports. I met the owner through Houston Baptist. It was a Christian organization that held camps throughout the summer. I worked with Triumph during the day and trained for basketball at night. At times I would even train during my lunch break. I made a couple of thousand dollars per summer and would save it. I was very frugal, strategic, and I lived far below my means. Before I knew it, August rolled around, and again I had no offers. At this point, I understood the industry. I knew that if something didn't happen soon, I would be at home until December again.

It was August 22nd, around 5 am and I woke in the middle of the night. Due to anxiety and the fear of missing out, my body would wake itself up. I checked EuroBasket, my text, and all other social media platforms to see if my agent had messaged me and to check if someone had signed. I also always checked my email for some reason, I thought maybe I would have a contract sitting in my inbox. This idea was farfetched, but optimism was my best friend. This particular day, I got a message from a random number saying that I had been selected for the Nigerian Men's National Team and asked if it could fly out by 11 am. I thought I was in a dream. It was now 6 am, and they wanted me to be at the airport by 11 am? What would have happened if I wouldn't have checked my phone on time? I don't know why I was surprised, this was normal behavior from a Nigerian. My resume was submitted to the coach a couple of days prior, but I didn't know when they were going to make a decision. I jumped out of bed and immediately started cramming my life into a bag. After hours of last-minute packing, I messaged the coach with confirmation that I would be coming and headed to George Bush Intercontinental Airport. I was headed to Buffalo, New York for the first part of the training camp. I assumed if all went well, I would be invited to the main training camp in Nigeria. Everything was so last minute I wasn't sure about many of the details. As the flight boarded, I received a message from one of my old friends, Bryant Mbamalu. Bryant was another talented player who lived in Houston. We played for rival high schools and trained together during the summer. In his text, he mentioned how he received a similar email that morning but woke up late and was running behind and if there was anything I could do to hold off the plane. I told the flight attendant at the gate that someone was on the way and she gladly helped.

When we arrived in Buffalo, we were picked up by the Men's

Head Coach, Alex Nwora. He apologized for the circumstances and gave us our itinerary. He also explained why everything was last minute. They had recently made a coaching change and he was the replacement. When that happened the previous team players from the years prior dropped out. I understood that getting a last-minute call meant I couldn't have been his first option. I told him thanks for considering me and that I would gladly represent my country. About 65,000 Nigerians were living in Texas. Of them, two were selected to play for the national team. I was one of them and it was a pretty big deal.

On the team, there were seven Americans in total and the rest were Nigerian natives (home-based players). As Coach Nwora pulled up to the hotel to drop us off, he explained that two guys missed their flight and two were already in the hotel. The guys were in two separate rooms, so Bryant and I split up.

Not only was I lucky to have been invited, but this opportunity also bought me time to figure out where I was going next. Typically, I would have been at home stressing every minute of the day. I hoped I would gain notoriety with European teams by playing for the national team. The next morning two more players were waiting in the lobby before we went to the gym. It was a mini-camp so the next couple of days consisted of weights, on-court training, and rehab twice a day. There were no rules or restrictions. It wasn't organized, he just allowed us to get in gym time. The practices were led by the senior players, some of whom had played in the NBA. Before we knew it, we were on a plane to Nigeria. I was excited to get the opportunity to see my mom, it had almost been a year and a half since I last saw her.

When we arrived in Nigeria, my mom was waiting for me to walk out of the terminal. It wasn't solely because she missed me, but Nigeria has a high crime rate and she thought there was a possibility someone could take me for ransom. Was that going to happen? Highly unlikely. However, it's true that Nigeria was dangerous. The first time I visited there when I was twelve years old, I saw two dead bodies.

We were assigned to spend the next two weeks in Nigeria preparing for the Afro-Basket tournament. Afro-Basket is a tournament in Africa where the African teams compete against each other. If I had to guess, I would say that we were probably the most unorganized of the teams. Our coach had put together a team in 24 hours and it didn't get much more organized after that.

The first night we got settled in, we stayed at one of the more notarized hotels in Nigeria, The Eko Hotel. Nigeria is a developing country, the hotel didn't compare to one in America but it sufficed. It was a nice hotel, very westernized. They had all the amenities; a weight room, hot tub, and pool. The food tasted great, but it usually gave us an upset stomach. Nigerians are cheap, we were convinced they were reusing the food every day and that's why guys were getting sick. We practiced at different times every day anywhere from 8-10 am. They would send a text out last minute and somehow expected everyone to be looking at their phone. It took us an hour to get to practice. It was only about 20 minutes away, but Nigeria just had the worst traffic. We had so many people that some had to ride in random cars. The gym was embarrassing, I couldn't believe they had professionals train on that court. I could see dirt particles all over from a mile away. There was no actual janitor, they just hired a guy off the street to sweep. The floor was hard, it was awful for the knees. Every time a player tried to stop, there was a drift due to the lack of grip. The gym walls were made of cement, which had holes in random spots where the hot air seeped in. After every practice, we would be leaking with sweat. We weren't able to practice with a FIBA regulated ball for two weeks, for some reason no one had them and Nigeria wasn't the country where you could go to the store and get a ball of that caliber. They had us playing with a ripped-up ball that guys used outside. Almost every player's first shot was an airball due to the inconsistency of the shape of the ball. We realized how spoiled we were because we never heard a complaint from any of the home based players. There were twenty of them and only five would make the team. The entire first week was dedicated to figuring out who they wanted to take. Once we did that, we started implementing a little bit of structure.

There were three coaches, two assistants from Nigeria, and the head coach was Nigerian from descent but lived and coached in America. Head Coach Alex Nwora had no idea what he was doing. He was by far the most unprofessional coach I had ever played for. He had favorites just like any coach, but if you weren't part of his favorites, he treated you poorly. We were all pros, we all deserved to get treated with respect. If you weren't one of his favorite players, he wouldn't call you by your name. He referred to me and a couple of others as "Yo" or "Bro." I questioned a million times where they had found him or how he landed the job. The best part of the training process was the media. Nigerians made Americans feel like celebrities. They would follow us everywhere and chant our names. They always had cameras on us, asking questions. We felt welcomed.

I spent time with my mom after practice or on my days off. We had two days off the entire two weeks we were there. On the last night before we flew out of Nigeria, we were finally paid. It was $100 US dollars a day since the time we landed in buffalo. $100 might not seem like much, but it adds up, especially when all your expenses are taken care of. Along with our per diem, we received our team apparel and jerseys. I wore number 3.

The following day we took off for the airport, there were twelve of us all dressed identically. It took around five hours to arrive in Tunisia. The country was beautiful, although it was in Africa the people looked Middle Eastern. We had two days to practice before the tournament, so we went straight to the hotel and then headed to the gym. At this point, the organization became better. The hotel was one of the biggest I had seen. When we walked in, we saw the other teams, Senegal, Cameroon, Cote D'Ivoire, and others. Immediately, I knew it was going to be a great experience. Our practices were timed with about an hour and a half to get what we needed and head back. We put in plays that didn't work but it gave us some type of structure.

Friday, September 8th was the first game against Cote D'Ivoire. We drove to the gym in silence as everyone was locked in before the game. It was our first time in the main gym. We warmed up and prepared to play. The Nigerian national team president Ahmadu Musa Kida came in and spoke to us before the game. I didn't know much about him, but I had heard earlier that year he tried to buy an NBA team, that was the only incentive I needed for me to be fully attentive when he spoke.

Following his speech, tip-off went up as I sat on the bench. I knew I wasn't going to start but I knew I had a good chance to play. They called my name and I was the sixth man. I went in and immediately missed two shots. I wasn't upset, I needed to get my jitters out. The coach left me in, and I scored. I had some assists and rebounds. 30 seconds left in the half, I chased down a loose ball and my hamstring buckled. I didn't know what happened I just knew I couldn't get up on my own. My teammates walked me back to the bench and I walked over to the trainer. As time passed, my muscle stiffened up and I could barely walk. I knew I wouldn't be able to play the rest of that game. We ended up winning that game by one point and I crutched off the floor. As soon as I got back, I did the treatment and hoped that the next day I would feel better. I endured three weeks of two-a-days and I was fine. In my first game, when it counted, I pulled my hamstring. The next day instead of practicing I went to the hospital. It was mandatory by the management of the tournament. I found out I had a 2nd-degree tear in my hamstring and I would not play the rest of the tournament. It came down to what I felt was important. Risking myself in Tunisia trying to play or rehabbing so I was ready when I receive my contract shortly.

It was the middle of September and I had not heard anything about a new contract yet. The positive part was I was not at home sitting around with an idle mind. I was doing daily activities that took my mind from the real stress. We continued to play Mali, Republic of Congo, Cameroon, Senegal, and Tunisia in the finals. The Tunisian team was unlike any other team in the tournament. They played like Europeans, finding the best shot every time and playing together while the other teams in the league played fast, off athleticism, and selfish. I knew it would be a tough match, but I thought we had a chance.

In that particular game the gym was fully packed. Fans were yelling, screaming, and blowing horns. It was most memorable to me because I hadn't played in an atmosphere quite that exciting. We took them down to the wire, but they were deeper than us. We played six players and they played nine. By the time the championship game came around, we were exhausted. Tunisia won by 12; they won the gold and we won the silver. We produced the MVP of the tournament, Ike Diogu. He was very talented and had multiple 30 point games. He previously played in the NBA and in China. We flew back to Nigeria to partake in some media sessions they set up for us before going back home.

Playing for my country was one of the most memorable and meaningful experiences in my life. From waking up with a random message, to attending a training camp, to then getting a 2nd-degree tear in my hamstring. Every bit of it was worth it. I had teammates who after a short period of time turned into brothers. Playing for the Nigerian Men's National Team meant the world to my family and me. Given the circumstances, I would do it all over again.

2017 Nigerians Men's National Team. (Anthony Odunsi #3)

Anthony Odunsi (#3) drives to the basket against Tunisian player in Championship game of 2017 Afro Basket Games.

CHAPTER 19
FRANCE

I flew back to Houston, Texas on September 23rd. As soon as I returned, I contacted my athletic trainer and told him everything. I didn't know how serious hamstring injuries could be, but he walked me through a timeline of how long it would take for me to recover. It had been weeks since I spoke to my agent, so time was on my side. Clearly, my agent didn't have anything for me, or he would have called. We went through three weeks of intense rehabilitation and then two weeks of on the court training just to get me back to normal. I didn't know how long it was going to take for me to find a contract and I didn't want to spend the money I made in Africa so I figured that it was best if I started interviewing for a job. I searched for job options every day for hours, the only good jobs were full-time positions. I needed a job that was part-time, so I could rehab and train accordingly.

I applied to a gym near my house called Orange Theory. They had hour-long circuit training classes. A friend of mine worked there prior, so I messaged him to see if they were hiring and they were. They asked me to apply online, I sent in my resume and received a reply from the manager with the interview process. I had to interview and workout in front of the manager. Not only did I have to meet the personality requirements, but I also had to fit the physical requirements as well. The interview process went well, she asked me about my prior work experience and if I have ever worked with computers. She told me most people get through the interview process, but it was the physical part they struggled with. Before the class, they wrapped a heart monitor across my chest to track my heart rate throughout the class. I passed with ease. It was a good workout, but it was nothing compared to what I had been through playing basketball. I told them I could start right away and they scheduled me for the next day. For the first week, I shadowed another employee. I took the early shift, so I could come in at 5 am. It was a very easy job. I answered the phone, handled the schedule, and greeted customers when they walked in. I enjoyed it but it only lasted a week.

On Friday in the middle of my shift, I received a text from my agent asking if I could leave in a couple of days. He explained that a player was injured on a team in France and needed to recover. I didn't understand at first, the player was still there so why did they need me to come? How could they do that? He told me that the team was looking for an injury replacement. When a player is injured, the team will look for a replacement. If the injury is small, they will bring someone in for the meantime. If it was a serious injury, they would send the player home indefinitely and find another import. My agent expressed it was only for one month. I replied aggressively, 'What do you expect me to do in one month?' There was only one game a week and due to FIBA rules, November teams only played two games. I didn't know how I was supposed to be successful with that amount of time, but I had no choice. I had to take it, hoping that after one month the team would either keep me or another team in Europe would sign me since I was already there. On the following Sunday I headed to Caen, France to play in the French Pro B League. I arrived Monday morning in France after a thirteen-hour flight.

Immediately upon arrival, I discovered that most people didn't speak English. Almost everyone I walked up to look at me like I was crazy. The general manager picked me up from the airport and we drove straight to the gym facility where the team was currently in practice. I walked in with all my luggage and watched them practice. The injured player walked up to me and introduced himself. His name was BJ Monteiro. He played for the club the previous year and led them to a championship. Immediately, I knew that I wasn't taking his spot and that this would be a legit one-month contract. He was their best player by far. He led the team in points and assists. After the practice, the team huddled and welcomed me. They introduced me and told the team I would be there filling in for BJ. It was a lot of weight to carry, but the only thing I could do was be myself. The coach and I left, picked up something to eat, and then went to take a physical. Upon arrival, all players have to take a physical to make sure they are healthy. I have heard stories of guys waiting all year long, finally getting a contract and then being sent home because they were hurt or failed a drug test. I didn't smoke nor was I injured. After I passed, they drove me to my apartment. I unpacked two heavy bags hoping that I would stay longer than required. The next morning, we had practice. The team did two-a-days, everyday besides the day before a game. Even on game days, they would make us come in and shoot around early morning. The first practice was all shooting and ball handling with a little 2 on 2 and 3 on 3 half-court games. The second practice was the same but more intense and more contact. We went full court and it was a bit longer. Both practices were about two hours, the second went longer sometimes due to scrimmaging. I had two weeks to prove myself, so I needed all the training I could get but it was tough on the body. The first couple of days I could barely bend down but eventually my body and game adjusted to the speed.

It was the day of my first game, I was nervous as usual. I had put so much pressure on myself to do well. How could I not? I didn't want to go home. The game was so mentally tough because I always felt I had to impress someone and that was exhausting. I was picked up around 6:00 pm by my teammate. We never spoke, he didn't speak English. We just smiled at each other. He drove me to the stadium where it was freezing but I was warm due to my nervousness. I walked into the locker room and saw a jersey that had different sponsorships all on the side of it with "Odunsi" written on the back. Pride filled the pit of my stomach, I knew I had to make a statement. I got my ankles taped, got massaged down in icy hot and stretched out. I felt like I was going to have a big game. As the warm-ups started I started dunking. I never dunk, but my intensity was high. My teammates were looking at me as if I was going to be their savior just like BJ was. We were all wrong. Within 13 minutes of game time, I had only scored 4 points. I played timidly and turned over the ball. I failed to meet expectations. When I got back to my room that night, I had a familiar feeling. I can't quite explain it, but it was that same feeling I had when I was in Utah sleeping with my window open. The same feeling I had when I was in Iceland and I only scored 2 points in one of the games. It was a feeling of worthlessness and a feeling of shame. That night I felt like I could count the number of minutes I slept. I knew my contract wouldn't be extended. We had another road game against Charleville, and I played no better in that one. I even sat at the front of the bench and my coach looked past me the entire game. I was filled with rage, I stared at my coach's bald head the entire ride home. I didn't have enough time to show my worth.

I wasn't going to dwell on my performance and I decided to take a trip to Paris and meet up with Chris. He was playing for another team in France and also had the rest of the weekend off. I took a three-hour train ride early that morning. When I arrived, I finally found peace. It was the first time while in France that I didn't have the pressure of basketball built up. I took an Uber to the hotel, a prime location right next to the Eiffel tower. On the way, I rode in complete silence. I was puzzled by the view, scenery, and ambiance of Paris. There were lights everywhere, people were holding hands and dancing in the square. It seemed like a loving atmosphere. Once I arrived at the hotel, I changed my clothes and we left. We only had the night, so we didn't want to waste any time. The hotel room was a storage room for our bags, we didn't plan to be there much.

First, we were to meet up with one of Chris's teammates. He had two female friends who were coming with him as well. He had a wife and a kid back in America, but I was not one to judge. We all went to eat, and when the bill came Chris and his teammate split it. Usually, when Chris's teammate wasn't there he would just pay for me. While some people would love the treatment, it bothered me that I couldn't help more. My contracts were small, I didn't have money to showboat around with. Every place we went that night either Chris or his teammate would cover the tab and every time that happened, I lost a piece of my dignity. We stayed out all night and got back to the hotel around 7 am. My train left at 9 am, so I just stayed awake until I left.

Sitting in my train seat I exhaled from exhaustion. Not from the night, but from the stress I knew I was heading back to. Reality set in and instead of sleeping, I tried to figure out what my next move would be. I played two games. BJ was returning, and I needed to find another home. In Europe, you're only as good as your last season, but for me, it was my last game due to my situation. I knew no one would sign a player that had two games with a combined 15 minutes. Due to the FIBA window, the next two weeks would just be practice and no games. They strategically told BJ to wait until this time to get his knee drained so he could recover while teams weren't playing. FIBA's window was a two-week period where players could leave their overseas team to play for their national team. I dedicated the next two weeks to staying in shape and trying to figure out where I was going. My agent was hopeful he would land something while I was already in Europe. Two weeks flew by and there was no word. Finding a job isn't up to the player, there is a large amount of pressure put on the agent and that's why finding an agent that has your best interest is important. I am not sure how many teams my agent called or spoke to, all I could do is hope he was doing his job.

After my contract was up, I stayed in France for another month. I went to Gravelines where Chris was playing. This bought me another month. The best option a player had was to be in Europe when looking to change teams. Teams were cheap and didn't want to spend money on flights. I have heard stories, how players will fly before the season because they know the odds are higher for them if they are closer. My agent and I knew it was in my best interest if I stayed, so I did. Chris was more reserved than me. He didn't want to ask his coach for me to use the facilities, so I asked for myself and the coach agreed. I had to stay in shape in case I got a call. When his team would practice, I would lift weights, and then I would stick around an hour to shoot. He hated the fact that he couldn't go straight home, but he made that sacrifice for me and rebounded. It was hard, I wasn't getting paid, I was just wearing out my body while being optimistic for an opportunity. The worst was when he would go on the road, I would be by myself in one of the most boring cities in France. Not to mention the weather conditions were horrible in the winter, it was truly a depressing experience.

After weeks of no news, I flew home later that month. Immediately I went into hiding. I grew depressed and angry again. I would sit in a dark room for hours and think. I questioned if I was even good anymore. The game was destroying my confidence. I would hide from people because I didn't want them to ask me what I was doing or where I was playing. I was an athlete and the person many people looked up to. I was the "professional athlete," but I was making less than all my corporate working friends. I was halfway through my second year and I had not signed a full contract yet. After weeks of isolating myself, I decided one evening to go to a friend's house for a little get-together. I faked the entire time as if I was having fun. It had been so long, everyone asked how basketball was and where I was going next? I answered everyone in confidence but subconsciously only I knew what my situation was. All people ever saw was me in different cities, and different countries. They didn't know the internal pain I endured and hid behind on social media.

I drove home around midnight. While I was on the freeway, I randomly heard two voices in my ear. They were the corrupt voices that I heard before but for some reason this time they appeared to be louder. One voice told me to drive off the freeway and end my pain. The other voice told me to stop because there was more to life. **That night I almost ended my life because of basketball. That is also the day I got my next "wake up call."** There was a perception I would try to upkeep as a professional basketball player. People always put me on a pedal stool, talking about how many countries I had been to, how many people I had met, and how talented I was to be able to do those things. To the public it was the American dream, I got to travel and do what I loved for a living. For me, the constant pressure and uncertainty of the industry caught up to me and I wanted it to end, forever.

Anthony Odunsi (#16) participating in the French Pro B League for Caen Basketball Club

Anthony Odunsi's French Pro B Jersey

CHAPTER 20
AUSTRALIA

My old teammate reached out to me to help him workout. He had signed to play in Australia, and he had not touched a ball in six months. Originally, after his graduation, he hung up his sneakers. But after six months of the "9-5" corporate life, he decided to come out of retirement. He said he got bored of doing the same thing every day and he needed a change. He knew I was a hard worker and that I would push him, so I worked him out every day for three weeks to prepare him.

As for me, I didn't know what to do, I felt I had exhausted all my options. I knew once I left Europe, I wouldn't get an offer to come back, so I decided to look into the Australian market. It was a unique market, and a lot of agents had no contacts over there. I wasn't known for quitting. I had to keep trying because if I gave up, I would be subdued to failure no matter what. The Australian season was opposite to Europe. It ran from March until August which gave me time to see if there were any opportunities left. Australia had seven different leagues running throughout the summer. One night, I wrote down the names of all the teams in those leagues. I looked up their coaches on Google and then added them on Facebook. Once they accepted my request, I would message them on Facebook and wait for a reply. I sent hundreds of messages and either didn't get a reply or received a response that they had already signed someone. Due to the visa process taking so long, teams would sign players early. By January most teams already had their rosters set and were in the process of acquiring the paperwork. The process of messaging was humbling, to put in perspective I spent almost nine hours researching the teams along with sending messages. I didn't think I should have been doing the reach outs, but I never let my ego get in the way of me making money or playing the game I loved. Although it didn't work, I was at peace knowing I exhausted that option. It was getting late in the year and soon I would have to wait to get re-recruited for next season. Most European teams didn't make changes after December. Even if a player would get hurt or leave the team, they would just play as they were.

After messaging the Australian coaches, I noticed there was a mutual friend, an agent from Houston. He had recruited me initially out of college as well. His name was Jeremiah Haylett. I knew that he must have had players who played there in the past. I messaged him and told him my situation, and explained I was hoping to potentially get into the Australian market. He said he had a player who was a point guard who had an offer from there, but he didn't know if he was going to take it. I told him if he didn't, he could put me in for the job, and then I would sign with him. I assume he put me in for the opening because the next day I got a call from the Australian coach asking me about my background. A week later I signed to play in Melbourne, Australia. My hard work paid off, even when I wanted to give up, I didn't.

Australian teams had a list of criteria they needed for a player to get in the league and country. They had strict laws and regulations that made Australia one of the safest countries in the world. It was refreshing knowing I would be in a safe environment. I knew players who went to countries that were in hostile environments and war zones. I was happy that I could for once just focus on basketball. I was headed to a team called the Sandringham Sabers. Sandringham was a suburb outside of Melbourne right on the beach. I was astonished by the pictures that I saw. I was going to be living in paradise for six months.

Once my visa was cleared, I started getting emails about flight tickets and before I knew it, I was on a 22-hour flight to Melbourne. Not only are the climates opposite, but the time was ten hours ahead of Houston. I felt like I was in the future; I was a day ahead of people from back home. In America, we were going from winter to summer and in Australia, they were going from summer to winter. Upon arrival, I was picked up by a driver and transported to the gym. Australia had the most beautiful landscape, seriously, one of the most beautiful countries I had ever seen. English was the language of origin, so there was no language barrier which made it easy to acclimate. Although I was far from home, I never experienced being homesick like I did in other countries. I arrived at the gym and met my teammates and coach. My coach was young, bald, and in his mid-30s. He introduced me to one of my teammates I would be living with. He was Sudanese but held an Australian passport. His name was Mackuei Poundak but we called him "P Black" for short. The name was given to him before our meeting, but he was one of the darkest guys I ever saw, therefore the name was warranted. My other teammate missed his flight but would be coming in the following day. They had two cars for us, one for each of the Americans. Since my teammate wasn't there, they gave me my car, then my teammate and I drove to the house. The car was old and beaten-up, but it got the job done. Aussies drove on the opposite side of the road, not only that but their steering wheel was on the other side as well. My first time driving, I ran over three curbs but eventually it became second nature. We pulled up to a nice house in the suburbs about five minutes away from the water. There were three bedrooms, televisions, and a washer and dryer. This was the first country to actually use dryers.

Early the next morning the other import, Trey was dropped off at the house. The three of us immediately got along. We all played different positions so that helped as well. We only practiced twice a week but did individuals the other days. Individuals were optional, the coach was very relaxed. We would play in two scrimmage matches, then ran right into the first round of games. Before the season my coach always talked about me being a facilitator which confused me, but I went along with it to get the job. Most teams wanted Americans to come in and score but yet somehow, I got on a team where the coach wanted me to be like John Stockton. I was strong and quick, and this guy wanted me to pass. I didn't complain, after everything I went through to get to that point, I was just going to be appreciative of the opportunity.

After our third day in Australia, we had a scrimmage. The coach barely played us due to jetlag, but I had a chance to see what the competition was like. It was very impressive. We also played one of the best teams in the league which had one of the best guards. Teams lacked structure due to only practicing twice a week, but the talent level was pretty good. The average Australian was better than most domestic players from other countries. By the time the next scrimmage came around, I was a lot more comfortable. I had 30 points and I knew I was destined for a great season.

Despite the contract I signed, I was enjoying Australia. I walked and did more exploring than I had done anywhere else. The people were friendly, I figured out early that Australia unlike the Southern States of the U.S. aren't racist. I am sure there is racism there, but it was much more discrete than what I was used to. In fact, as an American, I felt idolized. Anytime I went out, I would always have women starring or asking to hear my accent. Australia hit home with me immediately, I had no reservations.

Up until that point, everything seemed smooth, but nothing ever stayed that way for me. Something always had to come up. Our other import was different from me, he didn't necessarily get it. I was raised around white people; I knew how some of them judged and stereotyped minorities. If I ever felt a type of way about what went on with our team, I would talk about it amongst the people in the house or just bottle it in. Trey on the other hand was loud, he used to curse at the Australians if they were doing stuff wrong. He would talk back to the coach if he did something he didn't like. He smoked cigarettes and would walk around smelling like an ashtray. Worst of all he wasn't playing well. He could never make it through practice, he always stopped half-way through and grabbed ice. He was a liability, and it was becoming apparent. Often times, if a player seems detrimental but they are helping the team win, teams will keep the player and then the following year not re-sign them. But if you were detrimental and not holding up your part on the court, it is a call for early termination.

We played our third game of the season on a Saturday. It was a day game and those were my favorites. I hated the suspense of waiting all day to play, so I was always thankful for the ones during the day. We were playing against a very talented team, the Dandenong Rangers. They had two Australians who were getting paid well in the NBL; Reese Vague, and Anthony Drimic. The NBL was Australia's Premier League. I played against Anthony when I was a freshman, he was at Boise State while I was at Utah. He dominated the game, it was pretty impressive from another freshman. We had a talented team despite having a coach who didn't know what he was doing nor did he have the respect from the players. One day he would try to be our friend and the next day he would try to be a disciplinarian. It didn't work well. I didn't know much about Reese, but I found out more about his play that day. He made a fool out of Trey. Because Trey couldn't physically handle his own, he took it out on other people, and he started spazzing in the middle of the game. I have been accustomed to many players which led me to see a lot of things but never have I seen a spaz session like that. Trey was cursing, yelling, and belittling everyone. We were all so confused about what transpired for him to react that way. We lost the game and as we walked into the locker room he started yelling even more. He exploded and stormed out with his keys.

That following Monday Trey and I were called to the gym at 7 am. We were told to be there sharp and ready to workout. They immediately split us up, they told me to go upstairs and told Trey to stay downstairs and workout in front of the GM and president. Something wasn't right, *why was the GM and president at the stadium that early in the morning?* I questioned. That was my first time seeing the president in person, I knew what he looked like from a picture. When I went into the room upstairs the coach talked to me about my role. He said I was scoring too much, and they had other players to do that. I was leading the team in scoring and assists at the time. I was confused but I realized there was something internal going on with this club. I had met an Australian girl, who also played basketball, and she mentioned how certain basketball clubs look out for their own. They would bring out Americans but wouldn't treat them like they were supposed to whether it was playing time or pay. She advised that Sandringham could be like that, but it was too early to know.

After my meeting, I left to get an acupuncture across the street at the rehabilitation center. Sandringham had a great rehab facility right behind the gymnasium. As I walked out, I saw Trey limping and the GM and president walking up to the room I was just in. I still didn't think anything of it, I thought at the most they would talk to him about his behavior. After rehab as I pulled into my driveway, I received a call from my coach. He said he cut Trey and they were going to send him back to the states the next day. He said he had never been disrespected like that in his life and the organization would not condone that behavior. I have never been on a team where someone was cut, I couldn't believe it. I knew how hard it was for Americans to find basketball jobs, so I knew this would probably be the end for him. The coach begged me to help get his gear and car keys from him, so he didn't do anything reckless with the car before he left. I wasn't about to monitor him like a kid, he was mature enough to do the right thing. Trey was from Mississippi, and I'm not sure what Mississippi was like, but he told me where he was from wasn't the best. Basketball gave him an outlet and he took it for granted. Australia gave him a better life, more opportunity, not only for a basketball player but for an African-American. I hate that he will never know what he missed out on.

Life had to resume and I was nervous. I tried to make sure that I didn't do anything to cause them to cut me next. Although I wasn't getting paid much, it was still better than nothing. The following practice after Trey's departure, a new player joined our team. It was a guy all the Aussies were freaked out about, he even had my coach star struck. He was an Olympian who played in the NBL as well for the team that won the championship that year. It seemed like everyone on the team cared to mention it to me. He wasn't paying my bills, so I didn't care. His name was David Barlow, he was 6'9", and stronger than an ox. He was supposed to play in the New Zealand league but since they couldn't accommodate his family, he came back to Australia. He was a home-grown product of Sandringham, and they convinced him to play. We were one of the lowest budgeted teams in the league but someone had financial influence over him, but I was not sure who and quite frankly it was none of my business. He was going to help us. As practice went on, they started talking about him playing point guard. We didn't need him to do that, but that's when I knew that my coach had ulterior motives. From that point on we called him the "puppet" because we knew someone else; higher management was controlling him.

Our next game was in Tasmania, one of our few road trips of the year and our first with David Barlow. David was a first-class guy, he was a veteran who had played in reputable European leagues, and now he was playing for a team who had not won a game. He didn't complain about shots nor playing time. Honestly, he never really spoke or displayed any egotistical behavior. The staff put a lot of pressure on him. He was on the team solely to stay in shape. He was a role player and had made a great living doing so. The coaches wanted him to shoot every time and he wasn't that type of player nor did he possess that type of demeanor, he liked getting players involved.

We left first thing the next morning and caught an hour flight to Tasmania. We had two games to play back-to-back and once we departed the plane, we set out for the hotel immediately. We had a couple of hours to go rest, watch a film, and eat before heading to the gym. After our pregame talk in the locker room, my coach came up to me and said, 'Let's run the play for Barlow'. It was where I would come down at half court, hand the ball to David and let him go 1 on 1. The play didn't work and neither did his game plan. We lost the game, went back to the hotel, and had a team meeting. The bus ride was silent, no one said a word. We had become one of the worse teams in the league. We just couldn't find any cohesiveness, no comradery. In the meeting were four players and one coach. We talked about what we needed to do to win a game. It was late, no one wanted to step on anyone's toes, so the conversation didn't go as intended. The last thing my coach said before he broke out the meeting was, 'I'm going to have to change something and someone in the lineup, but I don't know who.' I knew my time was coming, they were going to cut me or bench me even though I was leading the team in scoring. I had a very good feeling that he felt I was the reason for the losses. When teams lose overseas, they immediately blame the Americans. Essentially, they fly us into win games and if that doesn't happen, they will either bench the import or change imports depending on the financial situation.

The next day we drove from northwest Tasmania to Hobart. The entire time, I anxiously anticipated the change coming. Immediately upon arrival, I went to the trainer's room to get my massage. I took a nap and woke up right before the pre-game meal. While walking to the restaurant, I felt a vibration from my phone. My coach messaged me and said he wanted to talk. I already knew what it was about, but I was going to make him tell me to my face. Instead of texting him back, I waited and asked him what he needed to talk about when I saw him face to face. He nodded as if we shouldn't have the conversation then and said he would tell me later. After we ate, I went back to my room to shower and get ready. He knocked on my door and told me the news I was waiting for. He said he was going to take me out of the starting lineup. I said, 'Okay' and continued getting dressed. Just because I was the leading scorer, didn't mean I wasn't the problem. There were cases where players were leading a team in scoring, but they were losing. When the player was fired, the team started winning. It's usually when the player is a chemistry bust.

Before the game as we were in the locker room the coach wrote the starters on the board, when the players saw I was not on there they looked at me with confusion. I always felt like the coach and Aussies had side conversations about me when I wasn't around. Throughout the pregame warmups, I was angry and frustrated, and I'm sure it showed on my face. My fellow teammates patted me on the back to show gratitude, but they knew it wasn't right.

As the game started, we were close for the first five minutes. After that, the Hobart Chargers had a substantial lead on us the entire game. I barely played the first half, embarrassed to my roots, I walked to the locker room with my head down. As I crossed by the import from the opposing team, he said, 'Why is your coach bugging?' While my coach was giving his half-time speech, I zoned off thinking that two things could happen, *I can let the coach defeat me and take my confidence away or I can ball out once I get in the game and show him what he's missing.* We were going to lose, either way, that was already apparent. The second half started and I was still on the bench. He did not put me in the entire third. At that point he was just trying to embarrass me; he thought I was the issue. He put me in the game at the beginning of the fourth and I legitimately went in with a tunnel vision mentality. It was like there was no one else on the floor but me and the rim. I didn't see or look at any of my teammates. Every time down I shot, and every time down I scored. Once the game was over, I had fifteen points in sixteen minutes. I still led the team in scoring after the coach tried to make an example out of me.

A coach can make or break a player. All the unseen hours I put in; I would never let a coach take my confidence away. The atmosphere amongst the players was bad, we were a bottom-placed team. While we got yelled at in the locker room, our coach said he was going to bring in another import next week. There was something we were missing and hopefully, the new import could help. After we left the stadium, I immediately texted my agent Jeremiah. Although this was the first job that Jeremiah secured for me, our relationship grew quickly. He didn't treat me like a client, but more like a friend. I could talk to him about anything. I genuinely felt like he wanted me to succeed and that was half the battle when looking for an agent. The other agents didn't care what happened to their players especially if they weren't highly paid. They would just collect their agent fee and keep it moving. Jeremiah said he would talk to my coach and see what was going on there because they were playing other guys who statistically weren't impacting the team positively.

As we flew back, they decided to give the green light on the other import. He left the states and flew in right away. I heard he was a center, so I didn't ask many questions about him. I went to the gym to work out one morning and when I came in, the new import was in the house. He called me "Pop" which was my nickname and only people from Houston, or those who knew me called me. Out of confusion, I asked him if he knew me. Then it dawned on me, the new import was Reggis from Houston, Texas. He lived about fifteen minutes from me. I was ecstatic. I didn't know him but I saw him at a couple of open gyms. Immediately Reggis, myself, and "P Black" were like family. Reggis was a 6'10" athlete and one of the most athletic players I have seen at his size. He could guard multiple positions and had very quick feet. He had just finished up a season in the G League and decided to come to Australia for the summer. He helped our team tremendously and we started to win games. He also changed the dynamic of our lineup and there were guys whose playing time reduced because of it. There was tension amongst the players and one day in practice a fight broke out. We were divided, most would expect it to be the Aussies versus the Americans, but it was the Australians fighting themselves. As a result, the coach tried to even out playing time, which caused more problems amongst the team. In the last couple of games, we found our niche, we accepted our roles, and I had to make the most of the time I played.

I led the Sandringham Sabers in scoring that year, after being fourth on the team in minutes played. I could have given up, but in a situation full of adversity I persevered. I never disrespected the coach, yelled, or talked back. I took all the lessons from my past and learned from them. I never wanted to fit the stereotype of what Americans came over and did in the past. The narrative will always be an American will come to a foreign country to try and get stats and put-up numbers. That's how we get paid and feed our families. I just wish some of these teams would look internally for the problem and not point fingers.

After the season, before I went home the coach and I had a sit-down. He told me I was talented and if anyone needed to talk to him for a recommendation, I should give them his number. He apologized and said he had people in his ear and that I definitely should have played more. Too bad apologies wouldn't help me get contracts in the future. I would have to hope another team would sign me after averaging only 16 points in a league where imports were averaging 22 plus. European teams looking at stats didn't know my situation, so I could only hope teams took the initiative to look at my per 40. Which was the number of points I scored in the number of minutes I played. That year I averaged 16.1 points per game in 26 minutes, the best per 40 in the league.

After the season we had a SEABL awards event to attend. It was a night dedicated to everyone in the league who received an award. For the players who didn't, we were still invited to come and have a good time. It was a beautiful setup, directly in the heart of Melbourne. The event was at a Highrise and it couldn't have been on a better day. The sun was out and there was music playing. We had the opportunity to enjoy the conversation with other athletes around the league. The event ended by 7 pm, then we went out afterwards. I didn't get home until 5 am the next morning. I saw another side of Melbourne that night that I would never forget, and I hoped to come back and play again under better circumstances.

Anthony Odunsi gathers to shoot free throw while playing for the Sandringham Sabres.

CHAPTER 21
WHAT I THOUGHT WAS
NEW ZEALAND

By the second week of August, I was back in Houston. I received a couple of offers from different countries before leaving Australia but they were nothing worth leaving the country early for. I flew back home to wait for better options. After two months of waiting, I decided to head back to Australia to be with a girl I was dating. She was playing in the main league for a team called the Bendigo Spirit. Bendigo also had a SEABL team called the Bendigo Braves. They were the highest budgeted team in the league by a long shot. After months of dating, I found out that her contract was larger than mine which made me put a lot of things into perspective concerning my basketball future. She and I thought it would be best if I flew over and waited in Australia. They had basketball courts, a weight room, and a gym all nearby. There was also a lot of opportunities to make money training younger kids.

Initially, when I made the decision, I thought I would be there maybe a month or two before I signed somewhere. My girlfriend and I didn't plan for it to drag out as long as it did. Days, weeks and months went by, and no substantial offers were made. Although I communicated with my agent at least once a week, I felt like every opportunity was slipping through my hands. I grew frustrated and took it out on my relationship. When I would get upset, I would shut everyone out, and not talk for days. The tension grew so much my girlfriend and I ended up sleeping in separate rooms. Eventually, everything spiraled out of control.

I desired to play year-round. Some countries like the Middle East and South America have shorter seasons, so what guys would do is play in one league then sign to play in Australia directly after. Half of the year had already passed and I knew it was best to start looking for an Australian team. With the season I had just the year before, I was surprised teams from Australia weren't reaching out. I had to humble myself and start contacting teams on my own again. It was a bit easier to communicate with teams since I was already out in Australia. The first coach I reached out to was a guy who had shown interest after my season. His name was Liam Glascott, he asked me to drive down and workout in front of him. I felt disrespected, I didn't feel I had anything to prove. Everyone told me that I needed to do it even if I didn't want to. So, I humbled myself and drove two hours to workout with the coach. He put me through a series of drills. I trained hard for weeks to make sure I was prepared. I knew in situations like this you only got one chance to make an impression. After destroying the workout, he still didn't make me an offer. Instead, he asked me to come to an open gym to play against other players who he was interested in. I was furious at his inability to make a decision, but I went to the open gym to prove a point. After hours of playing well, he still didn't make an offer. He later asked me to come a third time and at that point I told the coach I wasn't interested anymore and that clearly, I wasn't what he was looking for. When he finally signed someone, it wasn't even for my position, he needed a big man.

Every Saturday they would have an open gym in Bendigo and I would show up. They had another American, Ray Turner who married an Australian and lived there as well. Ironically, he was another Houston native. After a couple of weeks of attending, their coach David Hogan asked me about my plans for the upcoming season. He explained the league had changed its name from SEABL to NBL1 and they were adding more teams and more media to enhance the publicity of the league. David asked me if I wanted to practice with them in the preseason, after watching me play, he was considering signing me. I knew as a club they had the most money, so I did everything I could to show my worth. Anytime a practice was held, I went and I destroyed them. After weeks went by, I could see the coach was clearly leading me on. There were some practices where he wouldn't even look at me. He knew I was waiting for the offer. I grew tired and after one practice, I walked up and asked him his plan. He told me I wasn't a part of his first options. He had a group of players whom he had offered and was waiting for their reply. He said he gave those particular guys a date and if they didn't sign, then the spot would be mine. It didn't make any sense, why give these players so long to sign? If a player wanted to play for him, he would sign immediately. Clearly, that wasn't the case. That date passed and he never signed me. Weeks went by and he never contacted me. I asked David straight up what the deal was and he told me, 'If you have another option, you should take it.' I had spent months working out with his players and building a relationship with them. They needed a guard, but the coach insisted on waiting for guys who didn't want to play for him. What was even worse was, David unintentionally messaged my agent and asked him for some of his other players not knowing he represented me. I wasn't the player he was looking for and it hurt to go through that situation. It made me feel as if I wasn't good enough, although that wasn't the truth. It is known that the overseas recruiting process is grimy, but I expected him to be less egotistical. He was a player the previous year and one who never played. His career ended early due to concussions which led him to the men's head coach position after having no experience coaching nor playing.

I went back to the drawing board. I had no offers, no leads-nothing. Still, I went to the gym and trained because I was optimistic something was going to open up. One morning I woke up with some missed calls from Jeremiah. Usually, if an agent calls, that means it's urgent and some team is interested. He told me that a team in New Zealand (NZ) was interested. New Zealand is a superior league to Australia. All the talented guys from Australia went to New Zealand to make twice as much in a shorter season. I told him I would take it and the only thing I could think about was telling the Bendigo coach that I was going to a better league, with a better offer than he could give. But there was a catch, this was a better league but it was one of the lower budgeted teams in the league so they couldn't offer much money. The offer was lower than my first offer in Iceland. It was my third year in professional sports, and I was getting less money yearly. I started to think about my longevity in basketball. I started to think about what would happen if I got hurt or sick? Or what would happen if I kept playing until I was 35, then retired with no actual work experience, retirement plan, or benefits? These were thing most of my peers weren't thinking about, but I was.

There was a scenario I wrote down and it made me put everything in perspective. Imagine two people, in actuality, they are the same person just different routes in life. One is a businessman working in a corporate setting and the other is a basketball player, both just graduated from college and landed jobs. The basketball player if he is lucky would start at two thousand dollars a month and he would earn that for nine months if he didn't get cut or hurt. Considering he played well that season, he would lock in another contract for three thousand dollars, then five thousand and his maximum would be ten thousand a month. Which most players receive but I'm being generous. That's pretty good money. But the reality is he'll start to decline because of his age and his salary will decrease from ten thousand dollars to seven thousand, to five thousand, and he will ultimately retire because of the wear on his body. When he returns to his hometown at 34 or older, he will have to start all over, due to no work experience. He has to find a job with no actual skill set that he can offer a company, because he has been off playing basketball while others have been building their experience. Ultimately, he will be behind the curve. Considering he saved his money while playing he would have a decent amount of money saved for use, but not enough to sustain a living over time. Especially if there are kids and a wife involved.

On the other hand, there is the cooperate individual that after graduation would start at a salary somewhere around fifty thousand dollars according to SHRM. He would gradually work his way up every single year until he retires. After I understood this, I got my next "wake up call." This was the most important wake up call because understanding and applying strategy is imperative. The successful know how and when to make changes in their life and shift. I knew my time was coming. The time where I would have to stop doing what I loved and start doing what was necessary for my future.

I told myself after I accepted the New Zealand contract that I would play until a substantial job opportunity arose. But until then, I would continue to give basketball 100 percent of my effort. I flew back to Houston in January to spend time with my family. My mom had been in Nigeria for about a year and a half. Once I found out she was coming back for New Year's, I came home to spend time with her and prepare for the NZ season. Coach Tim McTamney was the coach from the Manawatu Jets. He coached them for years along with other teams in the league. He was very laid back in his conversations, and you could tell he was a player's coach by watching a film. A player's coach is a coach that adapts to his players, rather than making the players adapt to him and his system. He reiterated to me a couple of times that he knew it wasn't a lot of money, but he was going to give me all the opportunity I needed. He explained how he knew players need stats to get jobs and he knew as a club the lower budgeted teams had no chance to win, they were there simply to give guys an opportunity. He told me how he wanted to utilize me, and he explained that his point guard from the previous year led the league in scoring. It was self-explanatory what type of freedom I would have. I thought this was going to be a pivotal point for me in my career. I felt if I played well there, I could then have opportunities in more credible leagues. I was excited and had about two months to prepare, I knew I could get smarter and have a better understanding of the game. I watched tons of films, I dieted, worked out twice a day, and rehabbed just to prepare. I felt confident about the season.

As the date of arrival started getting closer, I noticed the coach became more distant. I have always been an analytical thinker; thorough, in-depth and calculated. At times I thought so hard. I'm sure I made things up to make sense of intuition. I knew something was wrong or something had changed, but until he told me something I acted as normal.

Things were a bit unprofessional; we didn't get our plane tickets until the day before arrival. When we arrived at our apartment, there were little to no amenities. There was no microwave, no utensils, we were supposed to have a car and that wasn't present either. There were two visas for short term residents, holiday, and working visa. The Holiday visa was for only three months, while the work visa was for a longer period of time. We needed a work visa to get paid but we were on a holiday because it was cheaper. They couldn't set up our bank accounts because the team didn't want to get us a working visa. There were many things they did upon arrival, that was unprofessional, but yet they expected us to come to every practice, game, and PR event. It was contradicting and I was getting over it. Without practices, walkthroughs, or films, we had our first scrimmage the day after we arrived. The flight was 24 plus hours long, and my legs felt like Jell-O. The game didn't count, it was just a scrimmage. Each team could have three imports. On our team it was me, Wally, and a kid who played with the team the year before named Kuran Iverson. He was former NBA player Allen Iverson's nephew. Wally, was also the brother of another NBA basketball player, Henry Ellenson.

At the start of the scrimmage, Tim asked me to come off the bench. I wasn't sure what differentiated me from the other guys, but I just let it play out. The scrimmage was sloppy, but we got a good idea of how the coach operated. We had a week to prepare for the first game. Just like all the other leagues, we practiced all week and played on the weekends. We started with practicing twice a day. An early session and then a late one. You would have thought the first practice was optional because Wally and I were the only imports present and half of the domestic players (NZ players) didn't show up either. Everything was unprofessional and it started to show quickly. We talked to the management every day about the amenities that we had yet to receive. It got really bad. Instead of microwaving, we cooked stuff in the oven or just got meals that we didn't have to warm up. Every day they would tell us it was coming and every day we waited.

My first game in New Zealand didn't go well, plain and simple. It must have been first game jitters, but I couldn't get anything to go. I turned the ball over, and missed shots I usually make. It was an all-around bad game for me. Later, one of my teammates walked up to me and said, 'Did you hear what the coach said?' I must have walked out early, because I was clueless. Allegedly he said, 'There are a couple of things I want to do with Anthony, and none of them concern this team.' I was confused, I couldn't believe he would react that way over one game, but that's how difficult it was to be a basketball player overseas. I slept it off, just to get worse news the following morning. Kuran said the other import that led the team in scoring last year was thinking about coming back and that our coach messaged him asking his current situation. He was in a European country waiting on another opportunity so he told our coach that if he made the right offer, he would come back. He didn't say who he was going to replace, but I knew it was me. Not only did we play the same position, but he always compared us. After I saw the messages as proof, I contacted my agent to dig deeper and see what the issue was. Jeremiah told me to have patience and let him handle it. That week in practice the coach couldn't make it more obvious he was going to make a switch in imports, not even a full week after my arrival.

Coaches had numerous of ways they would hint at a player who was getting fired. Some clubs would hold money, some clubs would fly another import in and have him practice, but the most obvious was when a club stopped playing a player. In practice he moved me from the starting line up to the reserves, then he played me out of position and had one of they younger NZ players take my spot. The worst part was my teammates acted as if that was normal behavior. No one ever came to ask me why things were changing. None of my teammates even batted an eye at what was happening, it was a cold world. That entire week we had two-a-days again. Although I knew something was going to happen, I showed up to every practice when many didn't. I kept my agent updated after every practice. I informed him about how half of our team wasn't showing up, yet the coach would yell at me. When Jeremiah spoke to Tim, he said the coach told him he was fully invested in me, but his actions were showing something different.

On the next game day everything came to light. We started with shooting drills and afterward he split us up on sides – starters and reserves. I was on the reserves, but he called some of the reserves to the other side to get in the rotation with the starters. This was done so that everyone; starters and reserves were familiar with being on the court with each other. After I saw he left me out of that rotation, I knew I wouldn't play in the game later that night. After shoot around my roommates went back to the apartment. One of my teammates came to my room and said the coach was cursing me out underneath his breath. The player said he was confused because he knew I didn't do anything. After he told me the story the first time, I went and got my phone, turned the recorder on, and asked him again what happened. I saved the recording for proof that others were confused about the coach's actions. I knew I was going to get cut, I just wanted to collect whatever documentation I could to make a case if it came to it.

That night at the game, during introductions the commentator called out my name, but I didn't start. I heard a gasp from the crowd, out of embarrassment drips of sweat rolled down my face. The first quarter went by and I didn't play any minutes. The second quarter went by and it was the same thing. He put me in at the end of the third. I ran up the court twice, somehow scored, and came out right after. He pulled me out for the remainder of the game. There was no explanation, just a smirk he gave that I could never forget at the end of the game. It's like he wasn't even concerned with losing. He just wanted to make an example out of me.

We had a long weekend due to Anzac Day. Anzac Day is a national day of remembrance in Australia and New Zealand, that broadly commem-orates all citizens of the country who served and died in wars. I knew everyone would be out of town with family but on Monday night I sent an email to the GM and president stating that I wanted to talk to them the following morning. I knew I was getting cut, but I also knew that was a coach's choice, not a club choice. I wanted to make a case to them about me being wrongfully terminated. The next morning, I walked down to both the GM and president's office. Jeremiah was on the phone for any legal matters. I had a list of things written down to make a case for me being wrongfully terminated. I was in NZ for less than 14 days, the coach wanted to terminate me but there was no valid reason why. The team, the management, and everyone else associated with the club got along with me, but yet the coach did not feel like I was the right fit. As a result, I felt it was best for the team to pay me out of my contract. I expressed to them how the recruitment of a pro basketball player worked. I told them I had other offers, but I turned it down to play for their club. Then I explained that because I had only played two games and for minimal minutes, it put me at a disadvantage with other teams. If I tried to go elsewhere, other clubs would flag me as detrimental. All they would see were two games in a country then no stats. These teams could pick players of any age, country, state, and city. Their options were unlimited however, it wasn't the same for players. To have only two games on a player's resume would hinder him. After I presented all the documentation, I played them the recording of one of the player's talking about the coach yelling at me for no reason. His mom was also on the board so that made things better. I told them how hostile of an environment this was for me and if I were to be fired, I should be compensated for being mistreated. They apologized, in fact, they both were very sympathetic to the situation. He said he would tell my story in the board meeting later that afternoon and let me know the verdict. They expressed their deepest sincerities; they didn't know all of that had taken place.

Later that evening they called and told me they could pay me a percentage of my wages. In that case, anything was better than nothing. I thanked the GM and president, they didn't have to be as kind as they were. Although the circumstances with the coach were awful, the club still handled themselves first class.

I decided after that situation, I was going to retire. I had enough, I had put a lot more into basketball than I was getting out and it just didn't make sense how others could control my destiny. I asked God in prayer before coming to NZ, to reveal to me what he wanted me to do. Whatever avenue was going to give me longevity to let it be known. I also asked him to show me without an injury. I had a friend who was injured and as a result, stopped playing. I wanted to retire on my own, I didn't want it to be forced. This was the only sign I needed. No player should be treated like that, just because a coach wanted another player. Before I left, I gave my brand-new pair of Nike shoes to one of the younger NZ players. I was done, I packed up my stuff and flew back to Houston the next day.

Anthony Odunsi (#6) drives to the rim while playing for the Manawatu Jets of the New Zealand NBL1 League.

CHAPTER 22
AUSTRALIA, I'M BACK

My flight was from Palmerston North to Auckland, and from Auckland to Houston. When I arrived in Auckland, my agent called me and told me not to get on the next flight. I couldn't believe what I was hearing, I thought there was some criminal activity happening in New Zealand and it wasn't safe to travel. He said he had two teams offer for me from Australia that same morning and they were both paying more than the Jets. One of the teams was in the NBL1 called The Diamond Valley Eagles. It was one of the coaches I reached out to while I was in Australia, but he said, 'He could do better.' Although I wanted to call him out, I didn't have time to hold grudges. NBL1 was a great league, the expansion of new coverage of the league made it more reputable. My ex-girlfriend also lived in Melbourne, things didn't work out due to the long distance but she was still one of my closest friends. The team purchased another flight from Auckland to Melbourne. I couldn't believe what had just happened, the timing couldn't have been more perfect, and I thanked my agent for all his hard work. Had I signed with Jeremiah Haylett out of college, I could have been making a lot more money, he actually cared about his clients. I knew God had something better in store for me, he didn't want my story to end like that, but he showed me the sign that I needed.

When I flew to Australia, I roomed with my ex-girlfriend for the first two weeks. Teams only practiced twice a week, so I drove to Melbourne and back from Bendigo until the team secured my accommodations and a car. Everything happened so quickly, they didn't have anything set up upon my initial arrival. Diamond Valley had their imports in a house and it was full. It consisted of two female players and two male players. Although I thought that was weird, it wasn't my issue. It was common, Australian clubs roomed their imports together. They ended up putting me with the team manager Shelly Reynolds. She had a nice house in Melbourne where she lived with her husband and daughter; and her son also played on the team. I wasn't too particular about living with a host family, I was a grown man and thought it was an invasion of privacy but given the last-minute circumstances, I couldn't complain. I told myself on my flight to Melbourne that God gave me another chance-another opportunity, and I should never take it for granted.

Shelley was the nicest woman ever, for the short time I was there she was like a mom to me. She washed my clothes, cooked, and cleaned while working a full-time job. I called her "Shelley the Legend." Her husband Mick was great, we never spoke much, just a couple of words here and there, but he always checked on me to make sure I was alright. They had a daughter, who I may have seen a total of three times during the six months I was there. She went to work and straight to her room. As awkward as it was for me initially, I'm sure it was for them also. I made sure when I could, I sat down and talked and built a rapport with them. I loved having them around, they were my family away from home. I always made sure I was respectful to them.

Diamond Valley was without a doubt a "boys club." They had all white players including the import. Teams usually brought in African-American imports, but they had a white guy named Logan. He was as athletic as they came so I guess the signing was warranted. They ran a lot of plays as most teams consisting of white guys would. I knew I was what they needed but I was sure I was going to be taking someone's spot, so not everyone would be happy. I just tried to fit in, it wasn't my team, I didn't want to trigger any divide. Within weeks, I got along with everyone on that team. That was the first time in my entire career I played on a team of guys where everyone liked each other and there were no team cancers unless they thought it was me. They had a bad team and up until I came, they hadn't won a game. I think at times they made it more difficult on themselves by running all those sets because they had talented individuals. In my first two weeks I couldn't play, I wasn't cleared due to a working permit. My first game, we had a back-to-back. Although we lost both games that weekend, the second team we played, we lost by two. The first time they played them they lost by forty. I wanted to have a positive impact that season, I finished my second game with 22 points.

We only practiced twice a week, everyday me and Logan would shoot and then hang out the rest of the day. I started to take it upon myself to be proactive. I would email the successful people I knew back home informing them I was approaching my last season and that if the right opportunity was presented, I would without hesitation retire. I didn't have any work experience, I knew networking and getting someone to vouch for me would be my best bet. I needed help from someone with leverage. I emailed almost everyone I knew, and for the most part, I wouldn't get a reply. When people did get back to me, they told me they could help, but never did. It was discouraging because I didn't want to have to settle for a mediocre job.

One morning, one of my old coaches finally reached back out to me. He had coached me in high school but because of distance, we fell apart. His name was Dane Hayton. I knew him since I was in middle school. He was probably one of the people I least expected to help. Given his background in adopting, I should have never underestimated his heart. He was a Human Resources Manager for a billion-dollar oil and gas company called Tenaris. He said he might be able to help me out, but he wanted to know how serious I was. I explained to him everything that happened in New Zealand and I told him I believed it was time. We spoke every day and I asked him about every aspect he could tell me about the job. After he told me the financial side, I felt it was time to make a decision.

It was the hardest decision I had to make in my life. I went back and forth a million times, but I knew that opportunity may never present itself again. But before I retired, I had to beat Bendigo. I was disrespected by David Hogan in preseason after he led me on by saying he would sign me but never did. There was one last chance I had to prove to him he had made a mistake. They had a point guard from the G League that was overhyped. He was athletic but he couldn't score and more importantly, he was a cancer on the team. I averaged more than him, although I played almost ten minutes less per game.

We traveled about two hours to play Bendigo and it happened to be on my birthday, July 7th. From the jump ball, I came out playing aggressively. I wanted to have the best game of my life. I despised their coach for what he had done to me. The game was close and as a team we weren't playing very well, but we stayed in the game. One possession, after I made a three near their bench I walked up to the coach and yelled, 'It's f'ing personal.' The game came down to the wire. Bendigo was up by two and we had possession of the ball. My teammate had the ball as he was looking for someone to pass it to, a Bendigo player ripped my jersey, and the referees blew a foul. I had a chance to tie the game. This was perfect, of course I was shooting the free throws. In college, I was third in the country in free throws made. Unfortunately, I missed both foul shots and we lost that game. For the first time in my entire career, on my birthday, I cried. I had let my team down, and I let myself down. I wanted to beat them so badly, it would have meant everything to me but that's not the way it worked out.

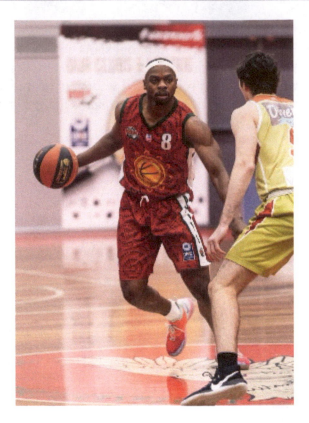

Anthony Odunsi (#8) sets up offense while showing off Diamond Valley Indigenous jerseys.

Photo credit-Rachel Louis Photography

Anthony Odunsi (#8) dribbles ball against Bendigo braves player while playing in Australia's NBL1 League.

Photo credit – Craig Dilks Photography

Chapter 23
The Last Dance

As the season came to an end, we were a couple of games short of the playoffs, but we made progress from their bad start in the beginning of the season. I was thankful for the Diamond Valley basketball club. For the amount of time I was there, I enjoyed the game of basketball again. The Head Coach, Grant Wallace, was a great human being and he allowed me to have fun through my last days, minutes, and seconds of basketball. The players on that team were great, all humble and hard working. I couldn't have asked for a better situation. Diamond Valley gave me an opportunity. They gave me closure.

On July 26th, 2019 I retired and posted this on my social media,

'I have decided for this to be my last season playing professional basketball. This was the toughest decision I have endured thus far, but one that has been exhaustively thought and prayed about. I have been very fortunate to experience the things I have, to see the places I have, and most importantly to build a relationship with the people I have. But an opportunity was presented to me with Tenaris (oil and gas) and it's something I couldn't pass up. Thank you to everyone who has supported me along the way, you know who you are. To all my fellow brothers still playing, understand timing, understand the situation, understand perception vs reality, and understand your worth. Understand you have a lot more to offer society than being an athlete. Basketball has molded me into the man I am today, the adverse times built character, and the quality times made memories. I am not sad it's over, I am happy and even more grateful it happened.

Papa'

I answered my final "wake up call." I fell out of love with the game. Everything I experienced allowed me to figure out what I wanted out of life and how I wanted to live. The life of uncertainty wasn't for me. I realized my energy should be utilized in another way. Basketball changed my life and I am forever grateful for it. It has allowed me to see many things, and travel the world, along with meeting many special people. In no way shape or form am I trying to convince anyone of anything or steer anyone in any direction through my words. I am simply telling a story of my athletic experience and allowing you to form your conclusion.

Use the game, don't let it use you.

I flew back to Houston and my life changed forever.

LESSONS TO LEARN

I want to leave you with some life lessons that I learned along the way. I believe these can help shape and guide you in your basketball career.

Up Until Senior Year of High School

- Listen to authority.

- The better grades you make, the more opportunities will become available from various universities.

- Be coachable and a good teammate, word travels quickly. Coaches will call random people to see what type of "locker room" person you are, and how you treat your teammates. If it's between you and another player, good character can be the determining factor.

- Don't worry about rankings. It does mean something, but it isn't everything.

- Get on a team that wins. Winning is better than averaging 30 points and losing.

- Play for a coach who has your best interest, not just the team with the most gear and exposure. **I was fortunate at my size to have coaches who allowed me to play with the ball in my hands (guard positions) even when I wasn't ready, I was concerned I wouldn't grow very much, and I didn't. I owe my transition to them.**

- Treat every college and university with respect. Answer every phone call, coaches talk and will know if you are a disrespectful individual.

- Understand that the decision you are making is a 40-year decision not a 4-year decision.

- Attend a university that wants you, not the university that you want. Often players will choose the biggest school. While I understand the motive, it's smarter to select a school that needs and wants you. A school that views you as a priority.

- No matter how good or bad things get, outwork everyone

around you. **I believe that is how I am remembered. I was never the most talented or athletic player, but I spent a lot of time in the gym when my peers were doing other things.**

- Never make a decision based on your emotions. If you are fortunate enough to go on a visit, have something to compare it to. Don't commit right after a coach pitches his offer to you.

College

- Wait for your turn. For most, there is no immediate gratification.

- Don't get discouraged, most freshmen take a while to acclimate.

- Focus on school, grades, and utilize tutors.

- Enjoy your time in college. You only get four years of it and it will never come back around.

- Utilize both summers of summer school. If the school is paying for it, take advantage of the time.

- Choose a college major that will always be needed and essential such as business, finance, tech, or anything in the health profession.

- Connect with your alumni.

- Don't burn bridges with your coaches or players. The road of basketball at some point will have to end, you never know who will be where.

Overseas

- Choose the agent who is best for you. Just because your agent was great for another player doesn't mean they will value you the same way. Try to choose an agent before June, this way he can start getting your name out to teams who want to sign rookies early. Remember for agents this is a sales job. They will all say the right thing and tell you, "How pretty you are," do your own research. **Remember, my first agent was an NBA agent. I was referred to him by an NBA client who toward the end of his career played high-level overseas.**

The agent had multiple high paid NBA clients. I was an overseas client. He made a lot more money from the NBA players than he made on me, therefore I was low on his priority list.

- Look at the agent's clientele, and if he has other clients of your caliber and from the same level school, he probably has connections at your level. If an agent placed a player in a country and on a certain team and the player plays well the team will build trust and will contact the agent for more players the following year. This is imperative because connections are everything.

- Create a great highlight reel. Teams are lazy, they will look at the first two minutes of the highlight tape and make a decision. All film needs to be high definition, make sure you display you can shoot the ball. The European game is predicated on good shooters. The paint is clogged, so players with the inability to shoot the ball don't succeed.

- The main signing period for overseas is from July to September.

- Your first contract is the most important, European coaches are very judgmental. If you play well, teams will notice, and you will have options the following years. If you play bad, teams will label you and you will have to take a pay cut the following year.

- Don't take a deal solely because of money. You are only as good as your last season, so you need to make sure you are in a good situation where the coach will play you and let you be a vital part of the team's success. **I waited for money for my first job and it almost cost me my rookie year. I had a low offer in Spain and I passed on it because I thought I deserved more money. I took a better financial offer in Iceland, but Iceland is a league a lot of European countries don't respect. I struggled to get a job after that.**

- Jobs for rookies are low, they try to get over on players because they are eager to play. Often times, teams will give a job to a player who is willing to fly himself overseas or a player who is already there. If there are two players who are similar in talent, they will give the job to the cheaper player and pocket the remainder money. It's always about cutting costs, it's a business.

- Don't be too picky with your first basketball job, if you get an offer, you might want to take it, but do your research on previous imports. The overseas game is tricky, some teams will fly an import overseas and treat him poorly or not play him. Stay away from those teams, there are plenty of teams who utilize their imports well.

- Stay off EuroBasket, things won't make sense, and guys will sign who are not better than you. It will just frustrate you, focus on your training and getting better.

- For many players, the money won't be all that much, get a part-time job. Do not blow the money that you have made overseas.

- Stay ready! The hardest thing to do is work out and train when you don't know when the call is coming. It will come and you need to be prepared.

ABOUT THE AUTHOR

Anthony Odunsi is a retired professional basketball player who was raised in Houston, Texas. Anthony attended Fort Bend Travis High School where he is the only player to play and start on varsity all four years. After his four-year stint at Travis, he signed to the University of Utah to play in the Pac 12. He later transferred to Tyler Junior College, Albany University, and then graduated with a degree in business from Houston Baptist University. In 2016 while starting on his Masters in International Business, Anthony finished as the third-leading scorer in the Southland Conference averaging 20.1 points per game, 4.5 rebounds, and 3.9 assists. He was named 1st Team All-Southland, and 1st team All NABC. He was also HBU Male Athlete of the Year. Following his collegiate career, he traveled overseas to play professionally in Iceland, France, New Zealand, and Australia. He has the honor of playing for his native home country of Nigeria in the Nigerian Men's National Team. He retired in 2019, after being afforded an opportunity in the oil and gas industry in Houston Texas.